SURVIVAL

LIFE IN EARTH'S TOUGHEST HABITATS

SURVIVAL

LIFE IN EARTH'S TOUGHEST HABITATS

By
Barbara Taylor

Consultant
Dr. Roger Few

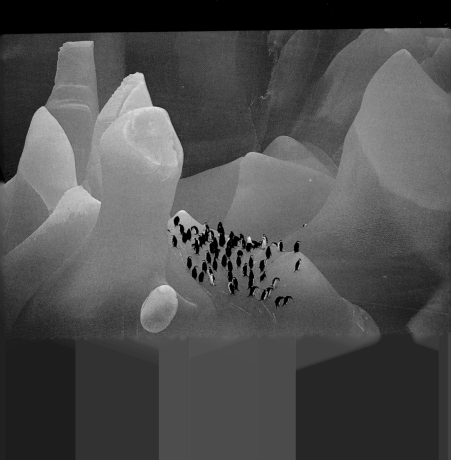

LONDON, NEW YORK, MUNICH,
MELBOURNE, and DELHI

Project Editor Steve Setford
Project Art Editor Peter Radcliffe
Senior Editor Fran Jones
Senior Art Editor Stefan Podhorodecki
Category Publisher Linda Martin
Managing Art Editor Jacquie Gulliver
US Editor Margaret Parrish
Picture Researcher Marie Osborn
DK Picture Library Charlotte Oster,
Gemma Woodward, Jonathan Brooks
Production Jenny Jacoby
DTP Designer Siu Yin Ho

First American Edition, 2002
02 03 04 05 10 9 8 7 6 5 4 3 2 1

Published in the United States by
DK Publishing, Inc
375 Hudson Street
New York, NY 10014

A Cataloging-in-Publication record for this title is
available from the Library of Congress

ISBN 0-7894-8848-5 (hc)
ISBN 0-7894-8849-3 (pb)

Reproduced by Colourscan, Singapore
Printed and bound by L.E.G.O., Italy

See our complete product line at
www.dk.com

CONTENTS

INTRODUCTION

The world can be a hostile place, but polar bears still stride across the ice in raging blizzards, cacti thrive under the baking sun, and mountain goats perch on wind-lashed crags. Experts like these amaze us with their survival skills. But just how do they do it? And what can we learn from these animals and plants?

There are living things nearly everywhere on Earth. The greatest variety is found in warm, wet places such as rain forests, where it's easy for wildlife to survive. But there's plenty of life in less hospitable places, such as deserts, polar regions, high mountaintops, salt lakes, and deep oceans, where day-to-day existence can be unbelievably tough. People find it especially difficult to survive in such conditions. Perhaps that's why we're so fascinated by the way other animals and plants manage to stay alive when the odds are stacked against them.

SEA ANEMONES LIVE ON THE SEASHORE, WHERE THEY ARE BATTERED BY OCEAN WAVES AND EXPOSED TO THE SUN'S DRYING RAYS.

This book tells the story of how animals and plants cope with such threats as blistering heat, numbing cold, shriveling drought, complete darkness, thin air, pounding waves, and crushing water pressure. It's a journey that begins at the ends of the Earth, climbs to the highest peaks, burrows down into the soil, dives to the deep-ocean floor, and carries you to a host of other extreme habitats. By the end, you'll realize that whatever our planet throws at them, animals and plants usually come out on top in the end.

For those of you who want to explore the subject in more detail, there are "Log On" boxes that appear throughout the book. These will direct you to some great websites where you can find even more information about the art of survival.

Barbara Taylor

STAYING ALIVE

I f you were left alone in the wilderness without food, water, or shelter, could you survive? The answer is probably not. We humans are pretty pathetic when it comes to surviving without the help of clothes, tools, and buildings. Wild animals and plants have none of these survival aids. They rely on their bodies, their behavior, and the natural environment to keep themselves alive.

Survival essentials

So what exactly do animals and plants need to survive? Well, life began in the oceans, and all living things still need the wet stuff to stay alive. Water is so vital because most of the chemical processes that go on inside animals and plants depend on it. Some animals contain an awful lot of water – jellyfish, for example, are 95 percent water, and even humans are 60 percent water. But animals

and plants are constantly losing water to their surroundings. So most living things – including people – can survive for only a few days without drinking to replace the water they lose. There are a few exceptions, such as camels, which can survive for weeks or months without water.

Food for life

Another survival essential is food, which supplies energy, and also materials for growth and for keeping bodies working properly and for repairing them.

Plants are lucky – they don't have to go searching for food, because they can make their own. Plants are living food factories, absorbing energy from sunlight and using it to manufacture sugar from carbon dioxide gas and water. This is known as photosynthesis, which means "making things with light." Virtually all animals rely on plants to survive, because they either feed on the plants or prey on plant-eating animals.

A very useful byproduct of photosynthesis is a gas called oxygen, which plants release

THESE MEN HAVE BROUGHT THEIR CAMELS TO A DESERT OASIS TO QUENCH THE ANIMALS' THIRST.

WEIRD WORLD
CAMELS CAN SURVIVE A WATER LOSS EQUAL TO 40 PERCENT OF THEIR BODY WEIGHT. WHEN WATER IS AVAILABLE, THEY CAN DRINK 22 GALLONS (100 LITERS) OF WATER IN 10 MINUTES!

THE GRAY
HERON IS
A WARM-
BLOODED
ANIMAL, ABLE
TO TOLERATE A
VARIETY OF CLIMATES.

as breathing and digestion, only work properly at certain temperatures. Plants rely on their surroundings to warm them up or cool them down. So do many animals, such as fish, insects, frogs, and crocodiles, which are said to be "cold-blooded." These animals can move into the sun to get warm, or into the shade to cool off. Cold-blooded animals tend to fare better in warmer climates, because if they get too cold, their body processes slow down so much that they become inactive.

into the air. Living things need oxygen to release the energy locked up in food. This happens in a chemical process called respiration, which takes place inside cells.

Warm- and cold-blooded
Keeping bodies at the right temperature is the last ingredient in our recipe for survival. Body processes, such

But two groups of animals, mammals and birds, have a big survival advantage. They are able to generate their own heat and keep their internal temperature constant, no matter how hot or cold it is outside. This is called being "warm-blooded," and it's one reason that birds and mammals can thrive in both hot and cold places. The fur or hair of mammals and the feathers of birds help to prevent the animals' bodies from losing heat to their surroundings. Many mammals can also shiver to warm up or sweat to cool down.

WEIRD WORLD
THERE ARE MORE THAN 800,000 KNOWN INSECT SPECIES, BUT ONLY ABOUT 20,000 TYPES OF FISH, 9,000 BIRD SPECIES, 6,000 TYPES OF REPTILE, 4,000 MAMMAL SPECIES, AND 4,500 DIFFERENT AMPHIBIANS.

THIS COLD-BLOODED TREE FROG IS WELL ADAPTED TO LIFE IN THE WARM RAIN FORESTS OF CENTRAL AMERICA. BUT IT COULDN'T SURVIVE IN COOLER HABITATS.

Adaptation

The place where a plant or animal lives is called its habitat. Over millions of years, living things gradually alter their physical characteristics to adapt to changes in their habitat, and to exploit new opportunities. The animals and plants best suited to the habitat survive, while others die out. This process is called evolution. It has allowed giraffes to develop long necks to reach high leaves, camels to develop humps for storing fat, and tree frogs to develop sticky feet to cling to slippery tree trunks.

The mudskipper is very well adapted to a difficult habitat – the mudflats of mangrove swamps on tropical coasts. This fish lives half the time in water, and half the time on land, as the

USING ITS MUSCULAR FRONT FINS, THE MUDSKIPPER CAN CRAWL OVER COASTAL MUDFLATS, AND EVEN CLIMB THE ROOTS OF MANGROVE TREES.

tide washes in and out over the mudflats. Like other fish, it has gills to breathe underwater. But the mudskipper spends more time out of water than in it, so it has developed the ability to take in oxygen through its skin when exposed to the air. It also has the advantage of bulging eyes on the top of its head, so that it can watch out for danger as it lies in the mud at low tide.

The mudskipper uses flicks of its springlike tail to propel itself over the mud in search of food.

Unchanged by age

Some animals and plants are so well adapted that they have remained the same for millions of years. The cockroaches of today are much the same as those that lived 300 million years ago. And the nautilus, a

THE TENTACLED NAUTILUS HAS GAS-FILLED CHAMBERS IN ITS SHELL TO HELP IT CONTROL ITS BUOYANCY. IT PROPELS ITSELF ALONG BY SQUIRTING OUT JETS OF WATER.

shellfish from deep down in the ocean, has stayed the same for even longer – some 500 million years. Although the dinosaurs died out about 65 million years ago, they were also very good at surviving in their day. In fact, these land-living reptiles dominated life on Earth for 160 million years!

Here, there, and everywhere

The champions of survival are the microscopic, one-celled organisms called bacteria. They were the first living things to appear on Earth, at least 3,000 million years ago, and they've been doing very well ever since! Today, bacteria can be found almost everywhere, including some of Earth's toughest places, such as in acidic pools and boiling-hot springs, on the deep-ocean floor, and in the frozen rocks of Antarctica.

People power

People are a fairly recent addition to the wildlife of planet Earth. Our earliest ancestors evolved from apes 5–10 million years ago, and modern humans (*Homo sapiens*) have been around for just 100,000 years. But in that time, we have learned how to change our circumstances to make it easier to survive. With our buildings, transporation, and technology, we no longer need to alter our bodies in order to survive. But the rapid changes we make to the world around us can endanger wildlife, because animals and plants can't adapt to such changes quickly enough.

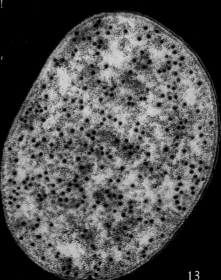

BACTERIA ARE THE SMALLEST AND MOST NUMEROUS LIVING THINGS ON EARTH.

KINGDOMS OF ICE

Extreme cold is a killer – if you go for a winter walk at the North or South Pole with no clothes on, you'll freeze to death in less time than it takes to have a snowball fight! The two polar regions, on opposite sides of the globe, are among the coldest, most inhospitable places on Earth. Amazingly, a few specialized creatures and plants manage to survive in these harsh environments.

Numb north

The North Pole lies in the Arctic Ocean, most of which is covered by a vast, floating sheet of permanent ice. Much of the land around the

POLAR BEARS ARE FOUND ONLY IN THE ARCTIC REGION. IN WINTER, THEY MAKE LONG JOURNEYS ACROSS THE ICE HUNTING FOR SEALS TO EAT.

Arctic Ocean – the northernmost parts of Europe, Asia, and North America – consists of virtually treeless plains and moorlands called tundra, where the ground beneath the surface layer is always frozen solid.

Shivering south

At the other end of the Earth is the South Pole, which lies at the heart of Antarctica, the world's southernmost continent. This huge landmass is almost entirely covered in thick ice, in places up to 3 miles (5 km) deep, and surrounded by frozen seas.

Seasonal change

Both the Arctic and Antarctic regions experience subzero temperatures, relentless snow blizzards, gale-force winds, and long, dark winters. The Antarctic is actually colder than the Arctic, with temperatures in some parts plummeting to an incredible –112°F (–80°C) in winter…that's more than four times lower than the temperature inside your kitchen freezer!

But it's not always gloomy in the polar regions – in the short summer, the sun shines most of the time, temperatures rise, and some of the ice melts. OK, they're still not exactly great places for a beach vacation, but all sorts of birds and mammals do move to the Arctic and Antarctic in summer to feed, nest, and breed. The seas are particularly rich in wildlife,

CHINSTRAP PENGUINS (SEEN HERE PERCHED ON AN ANTARCTIC ICEBERG) MAY NEST IN COLONIES MANY THOUSANDS STRONG.

from whales and seals to fish, squid, starfish, and tiny animals and plants called plankton.

Keeping warm

So how do polar animals survive in such hostile conditions? The key is to keep the cold out and to retain as much body heat as possible. Animals lose a lot of

WEIRD WORLD

ANTARCTIC EMPEROR PENGUIN CHICKS HATCH IN MIDWINTER AND SNUGGLE INTO A POUCH ON THEIR FATHER'S BODY, WHERE IT'S A COZY 96.8°F (36°C). IF THEY FALL OUT, THEY'LL DIE OF COLD IN TWO MINUTES.

THE ARCTIC FOX HAS HOLLOW HAIRS. AIR INSIDE THE HAIRS HELPS TO INSULATE THE FOX, SIMILAR TO HOW A DOUBLE-GLAZED WINDOW TRAPS WARMTH.

heat from their extremities – the sticking-out body parts such as ears, bills, noses, and feet. Polar bears and Arctic foxes have small, rounded ears and muzzles to cut down on heat loss. Some penguins have small feet and bills for the same reason. Many polar animals also have bulky, rounded body shapes, which lose less heat to the surroundings than longer, narrower ones.

Fantastic fur

Unlike us, polar mammals and birds don't need thick, chunky clothes to beat the big freeze. Instead, they have a dense layer of fur or feathers that keeps them warm as toast. Fur seals, for example, have 50 or more hairs growing out of every little hole, or follicle, in the skin, whereas we have only one hair.

WHILE THEIR PARENTS ARE AWAY AT SEA HUNTING FOR FOOD, FLUFFY EMPEROR PENGUIN CHICKS HUDDLE TOGETHER FOR WARMTH IN GROUPS CALLED CRECHES.

LOG ON...
www.EnchantedLearning.com/school/Antarctica

Cold-climate creatures often have two insulating layers. An underlayer of soft hair or downy feathers traps air warmed by the animal's body close to the skin. Over this is an outer coat of coarser hairs or feathers that keeps out even the fiercest gales.

B rilliant blubber

Fur and feathers aren't so good at trapping heat when they're wet. That's why many animals that swim, including penguins, seals, and polar bears, also have a layer of oily fat called blubber under the skin. Whales have gotten rid of their hairs entirely and rely on their blubber, which can be up to 20 in (50 cm) thick, to keep them warm. Blubber can be broken down by an animal's body and used as food when times are hard. Penguin blubber has yet another use. It acts as a shock absorber and cushions the impact when the penguin is thrown by the waves onto the rocky Antarctic shores.

S haring body heat

Ever huddled together for warmth on cold days? Penguins use the same trick to survive the big chill. A tightly packed huddle of penguins can reduce heat loss by up to 50 percent, with the birds taking

turns occupying exposed positions at the group's edge.

Polar waters

It's easier for sea creatures in the polar oceans to survive the cruel, dark winter than it is for animals on land. Beneath the protective cover of the sea ice, there are no winds and it is warmer than it is on the surface. Antarctic Weddell seals spend the entire winter under the ice. The seals have to gnaw holes through a yard or more of sea ice so that they can come up for air. Some scientists think that the seals use echo-location to find their breathing holes. This involves sending out pulses of sound and listening to the echoes that bounce back off the ice. Echo-location may also help them to seek out fish to eat in the murky depths.

Most polar fish, including Antarctic cod and ice-fish, have a natural chemical "antifreeze" in their blood, which prevents ice crystals from forming. (It's a little like the liquid we put in a car radiator in winter.) The fish swim happily through the super-cooled water, confident that they won't turn into blocks of ice. Polar plants and some tiny land animals, such as springtails (wingless insects) and mites

P lucky plants

Antarctica's a tough place for animals to hang out, but it's not exactly kind to plants either. Only 2 percent of the land is free from permanent ice and there's no real soil, although mosses and lichens still manage to thrive there. Lichens are partnerships of algae and fungi. They are incredibly tough and can live without soil, getting all the nutrients they need from

SOME ANTARCTIC LICHENS ARE AS MUCH AS 1,000 YEARS OLD

THE ICE-FISH IS ONE OF ONLY 120 SPECIES OF FISH THAT LIVES IN ANTARCTIC WATERS.

bare rock. Lichens contain high concentrations of proteins and acids, which don't freeze until the temperature falls below −4°F (−20°C).

S ummer bloom

If you're into flower arranging, forget about Antarctica – it has only two flowering plants. The Arctic, on the other hand, has more than 500 different species. Many of these plants grow in low, thick, round clumps called cushions. This shape keeps them out of the wind and helps them to absorb warmth from the ground. Because it rarely rains

(relatives of spiders) also have antifreeze chemicals in their bodies to stop them from freezing solid.

19

in the Arctic, plants need to hold onto as much water as they possibly can. Their leaves have thick, often waxy, surfaces with few breathing holes from which water can evaporate.

In summer, when the sun melts the snow and thaws out the topsoil, the tundra is ablaze with color as the plants race to flower and produce seeds in the short growing season. The air buzzes with insects eager to feed on flower nectar. Sundews and other carnivorous plants survive well in the poor tundra soils because their sticky leaves can trap insects, in addition to making food by photosynthesis. They digest the insects to gain valuable extra nutrients.

Even though the word tundra means "treeless," some trees, such as the Arctic willow, manage to eke out an existence there. But they are all tiny, their growth restricted by the brief summer.

Made for wading

Polar animals need to be able to move from place to place in search of food, so their bodies have adapted to allow them to

cope with the difficult terrain.
The extra-long legs of reindeer
and moose, for example, are
ideal for wading across bogs and
streams in summer, and plodding
through deep snow in winter.

The feet of polar mammals
and birds are often wide and
flat, with fur or feathers between
the toes. The wide feet work
like snowshoes, spreading the
animal's weight over a greater
area and preventing it from
sinking into the snow. Polar
bears, wolves, and foxes have
sharp claws to stop their feet
from slipping and sliding on icy
ground, while reindeer and
moose have sharp hooves to
give them a firm footing.

Some small mammals, such as
lemmings and snow

voles, use their feet to dig snug
tunnels under the blanket of
snow, where they can root
around for food, safe from the
attentions of most predators.

WEIRD WORLD

BY HUNTING IN PACKS, THE GRAY
WOLF IS ABLE TO TAKE A WIDE
RANGE OF PREY, INCLUDING
MOOSE AND CARIBOU THAT MAY
BE UP TO 10 TIMES THE
WEIGHT OF A SINGLE WOLF.

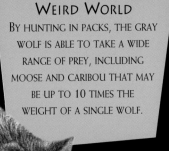

WOLVES USUALLY
LIVE AND HUNT IN
PACKS OF 8 TO 20
ANIMALS, BUT
PACKS OF UP TO 36
ANIMALS HAVE
BEEN KNOWN.

LIFE AT THE TOP

t's tough on the mountaintops – the thin air makes it difficult to breathe, the weather can be life-threatening, food is scarce, and it's treacherous underfoot. Plants and animals don't have the benefit of oxygen tanks, thick clothes, sturdy boots, and all the other equipment that mountaineers use. Instead, they've found ingenious ways to adapt their bodies to life at the top of the world.

GUANACOS LIVE ON THE HIGH PASTURES OF SOUTH AMERICA'S ANDES MOUNTAINS.

Up where the air is thin

On lofty mountains, the air is too thin for most mammals to lead normal, active lives. But some mammals, such as llamas, guanacos, and vicuñas (relatives of camels), cattle called yaks, and mountain goats and sheep, have special features to overcome this problem. They have larger lungs to take in as much air as possible, more red blood cells to collect the oxygen from the air, and bigger hearts to pump the oxygen-filled blood quickly around their bodies. Llama red blood cells live about 235 days,

LAMMERGEIERS SOAR ON RISING CURRENTS OF AIR.

more than twice as long as human red blood cells. The cells also collect oxygen much more efficiently than our own.

Thin air is not so troublesome to birds, which are naturally suited to high altitudes. Unlike humans, birds can replace all the air in their lungs at one time. This enables them to get the most oxygen from each breath, which is why Rüppell's griffon vultures have been known to fly at over 36,000 ft (11,000 m) – higher than Mount Everest!

Riding the wild wind
Although the air is thin at high altitudes, the weather whips it up into wild winds that batter the mountain-tops and

any poor creatures that happen to be on them! Animals usually find shelter when it's blowing a gale. It's too dangerous for most insects to fly, which is why insects on blustery heights tend to be wingless and simply scurry about on the ground.

But not all animals hide from the wind. Birds of prey, such as eagles, lammergeiers, and condors, take advantage of the strong currents of air that blow up one side of a mountain and down the other. These birds have large, wide, powerful wings and broad feathers. This allows them to hitch a ride up the mountain on the rising air currents without beating their wings much at all. The Andean condor has a wingspan of 10 ft (3 m) and can soar for hours on end using very little energy.

THE ANDEAN CONDOR'S BALD HEAD ALLOWS IT TO REACH INTO A CARCASS TO FEED WITHOUT GETTING GORE ON ITS FEATHERS.

PIKAS NOT ONLY FEAST ON THE SUMMER GRASS, BUT THEY ALSO STORE IT UP SO THAT THEY DON'T STARVE IN THE WINTER.

Holding on tight

Plants have also adapted to cope with the winds that lash the mountainside. Like Arctic plants, many mountain species are small and compact to avoid the worst of the raging winds. They also have long roots to anchor them firmly in the soil and draw up vital moisture. Mountain meadows are often full of these low-growing plants, such as saxifrages and gentians.

Getting enough grub

When the snow melts on the high mountain pastures, the plants spring to life and animals move up the mountain to feed. But things get much tougher during winter. Small, rabbitlike animals called pikas are kept very busy in late summer making "haystacks" of grass to snack on through the winter. A single haystack may weigh as

WEIRD WORLD

A GOLDEN EAGLE'S EYES ARE UP TO THREE TIMES SHARPER THAN OUR OWN. IT CAN SPOT A HARE 1.25 MILES (2 KM) AWAY, AND SWOOP DOWN ON ITS PREY AT AN AMAZING 89 MPH (144 KMH)!

much as 13 lb (6 kg). Large plant-eaters, such as yaks and mountain goats and sheep, can't find enough to eat on the high pastures in winter, so they move down the mountain to graze on the lower slopes.

Terror from the skies

Soaring high above these plant-eating animals are birds of prey, their eyes scanning the slopes for food. Golden eagles eat live prey, diving down and seizing rabbits, hares, and other small mammals with their razorlike talons. Vultures, such as Andean condors, dine on the corpses of animals that have fallen to their death down the treacherous slopes. Lammergeiers and vultures drop bones from great heights to smash them open on the rocks below. Then they scoop out the nutritious marrow inside the bones with a long,

thin tongue. They need a lot of patience, since it can take 50 drops before a bone breaks.

Surefooted on the slopes

Large mammals need to be agile and surefooted as they move around in search of food or to escape bad weather. Goats and sheep are superb at scrambling over jagged rocks and scaling steep cliffs. Mountain goats have hollows under their hooves that work like suction cups and "stick" to the rock. Chamois (relatives of goats) have shock-absorbing legs and rubbery hoof-pads for extra grip. They can leap 30 ft (9 m) down near-vertical rock faces!

MOUNTAIN GOATS CAN MAKE DEATH-DEFYING LEAPS BETWEEN ROCKY CRAGS AS THEY LOOK FOR PLANTS TO NIBBLE ON.

Hairy plants

The thin mountain air can't hold as much heat as the air at sea level, so the higher you climb, the colder it gets – especially in winter. Mountain plants grow hair on their leaves or flowers to insulate themselves, and to cut down on water loss in the strong, drying winds. Hair is also useful protection from the sun's harmful ultraviolet rays, which are more intense at high altitude because the thin air doesn't filter them out as well as the thicker air at lower levels.

The giant groundsel plants of African mountain slopes have a different form of insulation.

Dead leaves "lag," or cover, their trunks, in the same way that we lag water pipes to stop them from freezing in winter.

Legwarmers and winter coats

The cold-weather dress of many mountain birds, including Himalayan snowcocks, consists of extra-thick feathers, which even cover their legs and feet. Small birds find it hard to keep warm, but flocks of finches huddle together under rocks to share their body heat – like Antarctica's emperor penguins.

YAKS GRAZE AT 19,700 FT (6,000 M) IN TEMPERATURES OF –40°F (–40°C)

THE SNOW LEOPARD HAS A LONG, FURRY TAIL, WHICH IT CAN WRAP AROUND ITS BODY LIKE A SCARF TO KEEP WARM.

WARM, JACUZZI-LIKE SPRINGS KEEP AWAY
THE WINTER CHILL FOR THESE MACAQUES.

Mountain mammals, such as vicuñas and snow leopards, fight the cold by growing a dense, shaggy winter coat. In the fall, mountain goats and yaks build up extra fat under their skin to give them better insulation through the winter. The yaks' fur is dark, to help them absorb as much of the winter sun's warmth as possible. Many high-mountain insects are also dark-colored for the same reason.

Japanese macaque monkeys have surely found the most fun solution to the cold – they sit in warm springs that gush out high up in the mountains. A dip in the hot tub keeps them as warm as toast, even though they're surrounded by snow!

27

THE BAKING DESERT

The desert sun blazes fiercely in a cloudless sky as the temperature climbs to a fiery 122°F (50°C). The parched earth seems bare and dead. To live here would be like setting up home in an oven. Yet hot deserts boast a surprising variety of animals and plants, all superbly adapted to handle the burning heat and able to manage perfectly well with very little water.

Harsh facts about deserts

Deserts are places that average less than 10 in (25 cm) of rain a year. During the day, they can be scorchingly hot, but at night temperatures can sometimes tumble to below freezing. The landscape is mostly bare rock, or shifting sand that furious winds can lash into scouring storms. Doesn't sound very appealing, does it?

Camel survival skills

Well, it doesn't put off camels, which are famous for being well-equipped to deal with such outrageous conditions. The wooly fur on their backs shades them from the sun, but the rest of their bodies are almost naked, so that they can lose heat quickly. They also store body fat in their humps – not under the skin like most mammals,

CAMELS HAVE LONG EYELASHES TO KEEP AIRBORNE SAND OUT OF THEIR EYES. THEY CAN ALSO CLOSE THEIR NOSTRILS DURING SANDSTORMS.

which would block heat loss. If things get really tough, the fat can be broken down to release much-needed energy and water.

Being as big as a camel – or a kangaroo, antelope, or gazelle – also has its advantages. Large animals take longer to warm up

RED KANGAROOS LIVE IN THE DESERTS OF CENTRAL AUSTRALIA. LIKE MANY DESERT MAMMALS, THEY HAVE LIGHT-COLORED FUR TO REFLECT THE SUN'S RAYS.

stay cool in the desert inferno. As water evaporates from their skin, mouth, or lungs, it carries body heat away with it. Some

A CAMEL DOESN'T SWEAT UNTIL ITS BODY REACHES 104°F (40°C)

than smaller ones, rather like a full kettle of water taking longer to boil than a half-full one.

E vaporators and radiators
Being warm-blooded, mammals and birds can sweat or pant to

animals take this a step further. Kangaroos smear saliva on their bellies, legs, and tail to cool them by evaporation. Desert vultures and tortoises give this technique a yuckier twist by peeing on their legs! It may not

THE EARS OF FENNEC FOXES ARE DESIGNED TO RADIATE EXCESS HEAT AWAY FROM THE BODY.

sound too pleasant, but it's very effective.

Another way to avoid overheating is to make blood flow closer to the skin's surface, so that heat escapes from the blood into the air. Fennec foxes and jackrabbits do this with enormous ears that act like radiators. Their ears are packed with blood vessels, and because they're so big, there's a large surface area from which excess heat can radiate away. The cooled blood then circulates back through the animal's body.

WEIRD WORLD

WHEN THE TEMPERATURE CLIMBS TO 100°F (38°C), FENNEC FOXES CAN PANT AT UP TO 690 BREATHS PER MINUTE TO COOL DOWN. IF THE TEMPERATURE FALLS BELOW 68°F (20°C), THEY START TO SHIVER!

Too hot to handle

When desert animals find the temperature just too hot to handle, their only option is to get out of the sun. There are few places to shelter, so some ground squirrels use their long bushy tails like parasols to shade themselves.

Small mammals such as mice, gerbils, jerboas, and kangaroo rats find that the best way to escape the heat of the day is to dig themselves a cool burrow. Burrows don't have to be deep – just a few inches below the surface, the temperature may be as low as 77°F (25°C). That's still pretty warm for us, but it can make the difference between life and death for these little critters.

Desert birds such as elf owls and gila woodpeckers can't burrow, but they do take shelter in holes inside cacti. Not only are the birds kept cool inside the cacti, but the moisture stored in the plants' flesh provides the birds with a private supply of drinking water.

Don't waste a drop!

Water is precious in the desert, so the secret of survival is to not waste a drop. The hard, horny coverings of scorpions, spiders, and insects, and the scaly skin of reptiles, are like waterproof suits that stop moisture from leaking out of the animals' bodies.

The breath of animals that spend the day underground creates a moist atmosphere in their burrows, which helps to reduce the amount of water evaporating from their bodies. To cut water loss even further, many of them do not sweat or pant, and even their urine is highly concentrated. Seeds stored in the burrows act as

DESERT JERBOAS DIG BURROWS TO AVOID THE SUN. AT NIGHT, THEY TRAVEL UP TO 6 MILES (10 KM) IN SEARCH OF FOOD.

A HOLE IN A SAGUARO CACTUS PROVIDES A SAFE, COOL, MOIST HOME FOR THIS ELF OWL.

edible sponges by soaking up water vapor in the air. Kangaroo rats have such highly efficient kidneys that they can extract all the water they need from their food. In fact, they can go all their lives without drinking!

Drinking habits

Those animals that do need water have devised some clever ways of obtaining it. The male sand grouse flies up to 50 miles (80 km) in search of a drink. When he finds water, he soaks it up with his breast feathers and then flies back to the nest, where his chicks suck the feathers to quench their thirst.

Not every desert dweller goes to such lengths. One beetle just climbs up a sand dune early in the morning and raises its back into the air. Water droplets from fog condense on its body and trickle down grooves into its mouth for a refreshing drink.

The Australian native mouse has a similar trick. It arranges small piles of pebbles outside its burrow. Dew collects on the pebbles in the morning, and the mouse simply licks it off.

GIANT SAGUARO CACTI CAN WEIGH
AS MUCH AS A PAIR OF ELEPHANTS.
TWO-THIRDS OF THIS WEIGHT IS THE
WATER THEY STORE IN THEIR STEMS.

LOG ON...
explore/nature/deserts/deserts.htm
www.ontheline.org.uk/

Two-leafed wonder

Plants, too, have developed a variety of ways of coping with the water shortage. Welwitschia is a plant with unusual leaves, as well as a hard-to-pronounce name. The straggly leaves can be up to 26 ft (8 m) long, and are covered in vast numbers of pores to absorb moisture from fog and dew. The long, turniplike root anchors the plant in the soil.

Champion cacti

Without a doubt, the champion water storers of the desert are cacti. You could squeeze enough water out of a giant saguaro cactus to fill 1,000 bathtubs. (Don't try this at home!) Cacti

WELWITSCHIA'S LEAVES WIND AROUND THE
PLANT AND SPLIT INTO STRAGGLY STRIPS.

HERE YOU CAN
SEE THE WIDE
PAD ON THE BASE
OF A CAMEL'S FOOT.

have wide, shallow
root systems to soak
up dew and any rain
before it can evaporate.
They have replaced
leaves with spines, which
lose less moisture to the air.
Spines also help to deter
animals from trying to get at
the water stored in the stem.

S ubterranean water stores
Plants that aren't so good at
storing moisture may collect
water from deep underground.
Mesquite trees have incredibly
long roots to tap into water
stores as much as 50 ft (15 m)
below the surface.

Other plants set up
home at oases, where
subterranean water wells
up to the surface.
This is rainwater
that first fell on
mountains
outside the
desert and
then drained
through rocks
below ground,
before emerging
as a life-giving
pool in the middle
of the desert sands.

D esert travel
To cover the vast distances
between oases, large mammals
need long, powerful legs, while
birds need to be strong flyers.
Even short trips can be difficult,
since the ground gets hot and
shifting sand makes the going
tiring. Elephants, camels, and
addax (antelopes) have wide,
tough footpads to stop their feet
from sinking into the sand and
prevent them from burning.

AIDED BY ITS SMOOTH SCALES, THE
SANDFISH "SWIMS" THROUGH
THE SAND WITH S-SHAPED
BODY MOVEMENTS.

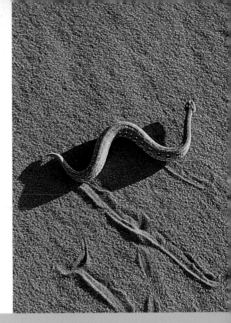

Lizards have their own range of desert footwear. Many have webbed feet, or toes with scaly fringes or bristles, which help to spread their weight so that they stay on the surface.

If the sand gets unbearably hot, sand lizards shuffle their feet, pushing aside the surface layer to expose the cooler sand beneath. Snakes don't have any feet to shuffle, but sidewinders

GROUND TEMPERATURES IN THE DESERT MAY EXCEED 158°F (70°C)

can hurl themselves sideways through the air. By doing this, only two small sections of the sidewinder's body are ever in touch with the hot, loose sand. Other snakes and lizards prefer to dive below the surface and "swim" through the sand by wiggling their bodies to and fro.

Staying alive is a big challenge in the desert, just as it is in polar regions and on high mountains. That's why wildlife often opts out of the bad times altogether, as you'll see in the next chapter.

ESCAPING EXTREMES

When the going gets tough, the tough hang around and stick it out. But the not-so-tough just hide or run off! Wildlife that's not physically adapted to deal with extreme conditions finds other ways of coping when things get difficult. Some animals head off to places where life's a bit easier. Plants and animals that aren't so mobile simply lie low and "shut down" their vital systems.

Winter snooze

Do you ever wake up on cold mornings and think what a good idea it would be to stay tucked up in bed until warmer weather comes along? Well, for some reptiles, amphibians, and small mammals, it's more than a good idea – it's a survival strategy.

the animal's body temperature falls to just above that of its surroundings, and its heartbeat, breathing, and other vital body functions slow down greatly.

In this inactive state, the animal uses much less energy. For example, hibernating . rodents called marmots

A HIBERNATING DORMOUSE'S HEART MAY BEAT JUST 7 TIMES PER MINUTE

At the end of the fall, days become shorter, temperatures start to fall, and food becomes increasingly scarce. Instead of toughing out the harsh winter months ahead, some animals hide away and go into a type of very deep sleep known as hibernation. While hibernating,

use only about 15 percent of the energy that they do when they're active. Many animals eat extra food before winter sets in to build up reserves of fat to use during hibernation. Others store food in their nests and wake up periodically for sustaining mid-winter snacks, and then fall back into their deep slumber.

Some animals hibernate for just a few weeks, but marmots stay dozing for as long as 10 months! When an animal emerges from its hibernation snooze, its body weight may have fallen by more than half… but at least it has made it through the winter.

CURLED UP TO MINIMIZE HEAT LOSS, DORMICE HIBERNATE IN NESTS OF LEAVES AND MOSS.

Going underground

Many plants have their own technique of avoiding winter's extremes. They shed their leaves and retreat underground, surviving as roots, stems, bulbs, and tubers swollen with stored food. As the weather improves in spring, they burst quickly into life and push their way back up to the surface.

RAIN HAS TRANSFORMED THIS DESERT LANDSCAPE INTO A RIOT OF COLOR.

they have just a few days in which to sprout, grow, flower, and scatter their own seeds before dying off. The new seeds remain beneath the sand – a hidden reservoir of life that will be awakened by the next rains.

Enduring drought

It's not just seeds that rely on rain to jump-start them into existence. The eggs of tadpole shrimp can endure 15 years of drought and temperatures as high as 158°F (70°C) while they wait for life-giving water. When the rains do come, the shrimp must hatch and grow rapidly to reach maturity and produce eggs before their desert pool dries up.

Desert bloom

Some desert plants also use a sit-and-wait strategy to avoid drought. One of the most extraordinary sights in a desert is when a sudden rainstorm conjures up a shimmering carpet of brightly colored flowers, as if from nowhere. Ten square feet of desert soil holds between 5,000 and 10,000 plant seeds, all ready to burst into life when the rains come. The water soon evaporates or drains away, so

Sleeping through the heat

Frogs and toads may seem odd inhabitants for deserts, since they have to keep their skin moist. The Australian water-holding

> ### WEIRD WORLD
> THE AFRICAN LUNGFISH CAN SURVIVE FOUR YEARS OF DROUGHT IN A MUCUS COCOON BURIED IN MUD. UNLIKE MOST FISH, IT HAS LUNGS AS WELL AS GILLS, SO IT CAN BREATHE WHILE OUT OF WATER.

ADULT TADPOLE SHRIMP ARE ABOUT 1 IN (2.5 CM) LONG. THEY FEED ON INSECT EGGS AND LARVAE.

LOG ON...
www.sciencemadesimple
.net/animals.html

frog burrows into the ground and sheds its skin, which it lines with mucus. This hardens to form a waterproof cocoon around its body that holds in vital moisture. The frog rests in this cocoon in a state that's similar to hibernation. When it rains, the frog breaks out of its cocoon and emerges to breed. Sleeping through very hot, dry conditions is called estivation.

Running away from trouble

Instead of staying put when it gets too hot, dry, or cold, or when food becomes hard to find, many animals pack their bags and head for places where conditions are more favorable.

Regular journeys like this are called migrations. To find their way to their destinations, migrating animals use inherited knowledge, familiar landmarks, the Earth's magnetic field, or the positions of the sun, moon, and stars.

Mass movement

Some migrations involve vast distances and huge numbers of animals. One of the most incredible is made by monarch butterflies. These fragile insects, with wingspans

WHEN THE DESERT RAINS COME, THIS WATER-HOLDING FROG WILL TEAR OPEN ITS COCOON AND SEARCH FOR A MATE.

HUMPBACK WHALES FEED IN POLAR SEAS DURING SUMMER AND MIGRATE TO WARM TROPICAL WATERS TO BREED IN WINTER.

of no more than 4 in (10 cm), fly 2,500 miles (4,000 km) from Canada each year to spend the winter in Mexico, where they cover trees in a living cloak of fiery orange wings. In a single colony of monarchs, there may be 40 million butterflies!

Mammals don't migrate in such numbers, but they can still create spectacular sights. On Africa's savannah grasslands, wildebeest, zebras, and other grazing animals make long treks to escape drought, following the rains to find fresh grass to eat. When they're on the move, migrating herds up to 250,000 strong may stretch for 25 miles (40 km) across the landscape.

Long-haul flyer

The longest of all migrations is made by the Arctic tern. This plucky little bird flies from its Arctic breeding sites to feast on the rich fish stocks in Antarctic waters – and then it flies back again, all in the same year! It's a staggering roundtrip of up to

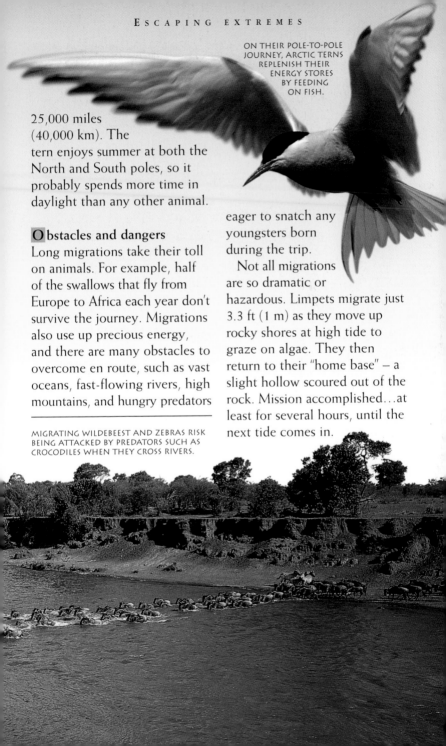

ON THEIR POLE-TO-POLE
JOURNEY, ARCTIC TERNS
REPLENISH THEIR
ENERGY STORES
BY FEEDING
ON FISH.

25,000 miles
(40,000 km). The
tern enjoys summer at both the
North and South poles, so it
probably spends more time in
daylight than any other animal.

Obstacles and dangers

Long migrations take their toll
on animals. For example, half
of the swallows that fly from
Europe to Africa each year don't
survive the journey. Migrations
also use up precious energy,
and there are many obstacles to
overcome en route, such as vast
oceans, fast-flowing rivers, high
mountains, and hungry predators

eager to snatch any
youngsters born
during the trip.

Not all migrations
are so dramatic or
hazardous. Limpets migrate just
3.3 ft (1 m) as they move up
rocky shores at high tide to
graze on algae. They then
return to their "home base" – a
slight hollow scoured out of the
rock. Mission accomplished…at
least for several hours, until the
next tide comes in.

MIGRATING WILDEBEEST AND ZEBRAS RISK
BEING ATTACKED BY PREDATORS SUCH AS
CROCODILES WHEN THEY CROSS RIVERS.

SHORELINE STRUGGLE

A day at the seaside is great fun for us, but for shoreline animals and plants, life is surprisingly stressful. They face a constant struggle to survive in two very different environments – air and water. They risk being dried out by sunshine and wind at low tide, and being battered by waves as the tide rolls back in.

Burrowers and borers

When the tide goes out, many animals on sandy or muddy shores – including worms, small crabs, and mollusks such as razorshells and cockles – burrow down into the sediment. They're

A PEACOCK WORM'S LONG, SOFT BODY IS PROTECTED BY A TUBE OF SAND OR MUD.

RAZORSHELLS BORE INTO SAND FASTER THAN A PERSON CAN DIG

not shy, it's just that below the surface it's always moist, so their bodies don't dry out. Mud makes a better hiding place than sand, as it has finer grains and holds water better.) Some of these creatures sift the sediment for tasty morsels of dead plants or animals. Others wriggle up to the surface when the sea returns to feast on its rich cargo of food.

A peacock worm doesn't just burrow. It also glues grains of sediment together with mucus to make a tube that sticks out of the sand. At high tide, it waves feathery tentacles out of the tube to trap drifting food specks and take in oxygen from the water.

The worm pops back into the tube when the tide retreats.

Piddocks seek safety in solid rock. These mollusks twist their shells to bore out a hole where they can shelter. Sadly, they can't detect other piddocks, and sometimes bore right through each other!

LOG ON...
www.bbc.co.uk/
nature/blueplanet/edge/

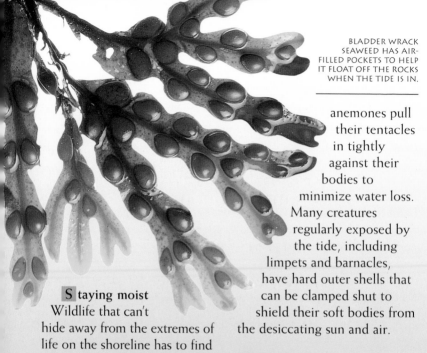

anemones pull their tentacles in tightly against their bodies to minimize water loss. Many creatures regularly exposed by the tide, including limpets and barnacles, have hard outer shells that can be clamped shut to shield their soft bodies from the desiccating sun and air.

S taying moist

Wildlife that can't hide away from the extremes of life on the shoreline has to find other ways of enduring the life-threatening conditions at low tide. Seaweeds have a slippery, slimy coating to stop their fronds from drying out. Jellylike

R ocky refuge

Pools of seawater that collect among the rocks provide a refuge for a variety of species, from small fish and prawns to

AN ANEMONE'S STINGING
TENTACLES PARALYZE PREY
AND PULL IT INTO THE
ANEMONE'S MOUTH.

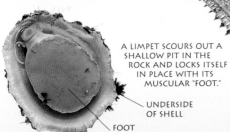

A LIMPET SCOURS OUT A SHALLOW PIT IN THE ROCK AND LOCKS ITSELF IN PLACE WITH ITS MUSCULAR "FOOT."

UNDERSIDE OF SHELL

TUBE FEET

FOOT

SPINES

starfish and seaweeds. These "mini" seas prevent them from dehydrating, but they aren't entirely risk-free places to live. Strong sunshine quickly turns a cool rock pool into a warm bath,

A STARFISH'S TUBE FEET ENABLE IT TO GRIP SURFACES AND CRAWL ALONG THE SEA FLOOR. TUBE FEET CAN ALSO HOLD PREY AND TAKE IN OXYGEN FROM THE WATER.

LIMPETS CAN SURVIVE LOSING 80 PERCENT OF THEIR BODY FLUIDS

so rock-pool dwellers need to be able to deal with a wide range of temperatures. They must also cope with changes in salinity (saltiness) and acidity caused by rainfall and water evaporating from the surface of the pool.

Get a grip
For seashore animals and plants, having a tight grip on the rocks is essential to keep them from being swept away as waves crash down on them.

Starfish and sea urchins have several hundred tiny, muscular projections called "tube feet" on

their bodies. Together, the tube feet can exert tremendous gripping power. Limpets, on the other hand, cling on with just a single large suction "foot."

SUBMERGED BARNACLES USE THEIR LEGS TO KICK FOOD INTO THEIR MOUTHS. AT LOW TIDE, THEY PULL THEIR LEGS INTO THEIR SHELL AND SEAL UP THE OPENING.

SHOALS OF GRUNIONS MATE AND LAY EGGS IN THE SURF WHEN THE TIDE IS HIGHEST.

In fact, there's a wide variety of gripping devices. Mussels anchor themselves using bundles of sticky threads, while goose-necked barnacles have a long stalk that glues them firmly in place. Seaweeds may use a rootlike structure called a holdfast to grip onto rocks. Lumpsuckers and clingfish are equipped with suckers to hold on when things get rough.

D ining at the strand line

Waves and tides aren't all bad news. At the high-tide mark, the waves deposit all kinds of dead and decaying plant and animal remains in a jumbled heap called the strand line.

Most shore creatures can't reach this delicious store of rotting food, but shrimplike sand hoppers are one exception. They hide under piles of damp seaweed by day and swarm out to feast at night, when the air is cool and moist. South African plow snails also visit the strand line, using their plow-shaped foot to surf up and down the beach with the tide.

E ggs at the top of the shore

A remarkable fish called the grunion lays its eggs right at the top of the shore, at the very limit of the highest tides of all, called spring tides. Here, the eggs avoid the attentions of predators lower down the

LIKE MOUNTAIN PLANTS, CLIFF PLANTS SUCH AS THRIFT OFTEN GROW IN LOW CUSHIONS TO AVOID THE FULL FORCE OF THE WIND.

shore. They may also develop faster on the warm beach than they would in water. They hatch in about two weeks – just in time for the next spring tide to wash the baby fish out to sea.

High-rise homes

The sheer cliffs that tower over many beaches offer safe egg-laying sites for seabirds such as guillemots, razorbills, fulmars, and kittiwakes. Vast colonies of these birds gather on rocky cliff ledges to raise their young.

Guillemots lay their eggs on the bare rock, without building a nest. The eggs are narrow at one end and fat at the other, so that they roll around in a circle, rather than rolling off the cliff and into the sea below.

Nesting birds may kill cliff plants by trampling on them and covering them with their dung – not a very nice way to go!

A bigger problem for cliff plants is the lack of fresh water. Rain evaporates rapidly in the wind or trickles away between the rocks. Some plants, such as rock samphire, store water in thick, fleshy leaves. Thrift, on the other hand, has narrow, needlelike leaves to reduce the water it loses to the air.

THIS COLONY OF GUILLEMOTS HAS TAKEN UP RESIDENCE ON A SHEER CLIFF FACE.

SALTY SURVIVAL

Most animals and plants need some salt in their bodies to stay healthy. But too much salt can disrupt their internal chemistry and, in extreme cases, be fatal. Just imagine, then, how risky life is for wildlife that lives in highly salty environments, such as oceans, salt marshes, and salt lakes. To survive, these animals and plants must avoid taking in unwanted salt, or find ways of expelling it.

Salt lakes and shrimp

There is one place on Earth where the water is so salty that nothing can survive in it. This is the Dead Sea, between Israel and Jordan. Its water is more than 30 percent salt – about 10 times saltier than seawater! Other very salty waters include the Great Salt Lake in Utah and the salt lakes of Eastern Africa, such as Lake Natron, Lake Nakuru, and Lake Bogoria. Salt lakes form where rainfall is very

BRINE SHRIMP PUMP EXCESS SALT OUT OF THEIR BODIES THROUGH SPECIAL AREAS ON THEIR LEGS.

low and rates of evaporation are high. Few animals can endure the harsh conditions, but those that are able to may be found in vast numbers, since there's not much competition.

One of the most common inhabitants of salt lakes is the brine shrimp, which feeds on algae and bacteria in the water. Brine shrimps reproduce very quickly – a female can lay up to 300 eggs every four days. If the water becomes too salty, or if its oxygen content falls too low, each egg develops a protective case around itself called a cyst, in which it sits out the hard times. When conditions improve, the hordes of shrimp hatch, providing hearty meals for the few salt-lake predators. These include some fish and insects, and several water birds,

FLAMINGOS GATHER ON SALT LAKES IN THEIR MILLIONS TO NEST. THEY FEED ON ALGAE, BACTERIA, AND TINY WATER CREATURES SUCH AS BRINE SHRIMP.

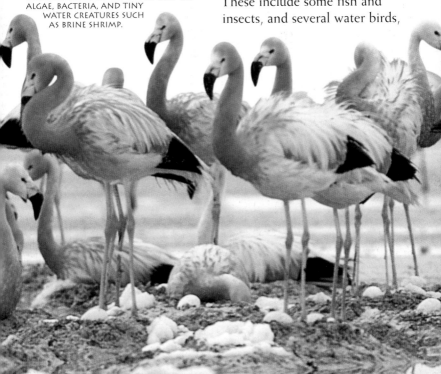

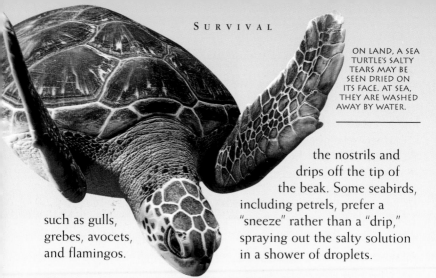

ON LAND, A SEA TURTLE'S SALTY TEARS MAY BE SEEN DRIED ON ITS FACE. AT SEA, THEY ARE WASHED AWAY BY WATER.

the nostrils and drips off the tip of the beak. Some seabirds, including petrels, prefer a "sneeze" rather than a "drip," spraying out the salty solution in a shower of droplets.

such as gulls, grebes, avocets, and flamingos.

Salty sneeze

Seabirds and birds that visit salt lakes have special glands just above their eyes to dispose of excess salt. The glands secrete a salty solution that trickles down

Reptilian remedies

Sea reptiles, such as turtles and crocodiles, also have to deal with the salt problem. Turtles can't sneeze out unwanted salt. But don't shed a tear for them,

EATING BRINE SHRIMP AND ALGAE TURNS FLAMINGOS PINK

PETRELS TAKE IN SALT AS THEY FEED ON FISH, PLANKTON, AND OTHER SEA CREATURES. THEY SQUIRT THE EXCESS SALT OUT OF THEIR NOSTRILS.

since they have their own neat trick – they "cry" extra-salty tears to regulate their salt level.

Rather than relying on tears or nasal sprays to get rid of salt, crocodiles use their tongues. Up to 40 special glands at the back of a crocodile's tongue produce a very concentrated salt solution, allowing the crocodile to expel salt without losing too much water. Strangely, freshwater crocodiles also have salt glands – perhaps their ancestors lived in the sea millions of years ago?

Big kidneys

Sea mammals, such as seals, whales, and dolphins, rely on their very large kidneys to control their salt content. The kidneys produce large quantities of concentrated salty urine, so they shed salt as they pee. Not surprisingly, the kidneys of river dolphins, which live in freshwater and eat fresh-water prey, are smaller and less complex than those of their saltwater relatives.

Fishy solutions

Seawater has a much higher concentration of salt than the body fluids of most sea fish. Without getting too technical, this

SALTWATER CROCODILES LIVE IN ESTUARIES AND COASTAL WATERS. THEY ARE SOMETIMES SEEN IN THE OPEN OCEAN, FAR FROM LAND.

concentration difference has the effect of sucking moisture out of a fish's body and into the ocean, by a process called osmosis. The only way that a fish can replace the water it loses, and so stop itself from dehydrating, is to drink sea-water. The fish then extracts most of the salt from the water and expels it through its gills.

GLASSWORT (IN THE FOREGROUND OF THIS SALT MARSH SCENE) WAS ONCE BURNED AND ITS ASHES USED TO MAKE GLASS.

Fish usually live in either fresh or salt water, but a few species can move between the two. Salmon, for example, spend most of their lives in the open ocean, but make long journeys up rivers to spawn. Eels go the other way, leaving their freshwater homes to lay their eggs far out at sea. In both cases, the fish can slowly alter their body chemistry to adapt to the increase or decrease in the water's salinity.

WEIRD WORLD
BEFORE IT WAS DISCOVERED THAT COMMON EELS START THEIR LIVES FAR OUT AT SEA, SOME PEOPLE BELIEVED THAT A CERTAIN TYPE OF SMALL BEETLE GAVE BIRTH TO LITTERS OF BABY EELS!

S alt marsh stars

Salt marshes and estuaries (river mouths) are coastal places where freshwater and salt water meet. Plants living in these places face a constant shortage of freshwater – they can't "drink" the seawater, and the only fresh water they get is from the rain. Because of this, they have become just as good at saving moisture as desert plants. Glasswort, for example, has scalelike leaves and a waxy surface to stop water from getting out. It also stores water in its swollen stem, like a cactus, and has a special membrane covering its roots to stop salt from seeping in.

M angrove magic

The mangrove swamps found on tropical coasts are home to remarkable trees that can withstand high salt concentrations. Some mangrove trees, like glassworts,

have a salt filter on their roots. Others may have special glands on their leaves that ooze out salt. Another bit of mangrove magic is to transport salt in the sap from the roots to old, dying leaves, which drop off the plant and take the salt with them.

So, the next time you sprinkle salt on your food to flavor it, remember how much trouble some plants and animals go to just to get rid of the stuff!

MANY MANGROVE TREES HAVE ARCHING "PROP ROOTS," WHICH EMERGE FROM THE TRUNK TO HELP BALANCE AND SUPPORT THE TREE IN THE TIDES AND SOFT MUD.

EELS SPEND 5–15 YEARS IN RIVERS, CANALS, OR PONDS, AND THEN TRAVEL UP TO 1,860 MILES (3,000 KM) TO LAY THEIR EGGS AT SEA.

ISLAND HAVENS

Dotted over the world's oceans are millions of small islands. Some are created when undersea volcanoes emerge out of the water, others when coral reefs become exposed and form dry land. The plants and animals that colonize a newborn island find that it's free from many of the difficulties they face in their natural habitats – such as predators, parasites, diseases, and competitors.

Colonizing new lands

The seeds and spores of grasses, ferns, fungi, and mosses are small enough to be carried to islands by the wind, as are some insects. Birds can fly there, and when they do they may carry larger seeds, perhaps stuck to beaks or feet or caught up in feathers. Seeds in the birds' stomachs also get deposited on the island in their droppings. Other seeds take the ocean route, drifting to their destination on the current.

Floating driftwood and rafts of vegetation provide traveling platforms for animals to island-hop. Lizards, tortoises, and other reptiles are hardy sailors, capable

COCONUTS CAN REMAIN ALIVE AT SEA FOR FOUR MONTHS, DURING WHICH TIME THEY MAY TRAVEL HUNDREDS OF MILES.

GIANT TORTOISES CAN WEIGH OVER 500 LB (227 KG). IN THE PAST, THEY WERE KILLED FOR THEIR MEAT.

of surviving long voyages on such rafts, with smaller creatures like snails and spiders for company. Most land mammals are too big for these trips, while frogs and other amphibians aren't good sea travelers since they can't tolerate regular soakings in seawater.

Island giants

Once established, island species must adapt to their new habitats. Some island reptiles – such as the giant tortoises of Aldabra, in the Indian Ocean, and the Galapagos Islands, in the Pacific – grow to huge sizes. Being large, with extra fat reserves, may make them better able to survive the dry summers on these islands, when there's

WEIRD WORLD

IN 1963, A VOLCANIC ERUPTION CREATED THE ICELANDIC ISLAND OF SURTSEY. FOUR YEARS LATER, 23 BIRD SPECIES, 22 INSECTS SPECIES, AND MANY DIFFERENT PLANTS WERE FOUND TO BE LIVING THERE.

little food or water around. But perhaps there's a simpler reason – with no predators to attack them, and no competition for food, the tortoises may have just continued to grow.

A more fearsome giant is the carnivorous Komodo dragon,

Survival through isolation
Islands sometimes form when landmasses slowly drift apart or when sea levels rise, separating wildlife from its mainland relatives. Some animals and plants driven to extinction on the mainland by competition

THE LONGEST-LIVING GIANT TORTOISE EVER RECORDED WAS 152

the world's largest lizard, which measures up to 10 ft (3 m) long. There are no other large meat-eaters on the few Indonesian islands where the Komodo dragon lives. The lizard probably developed to such a great size to fill the "gap" in the food chain, so it could prey on large mammals such as deer and pigs.

and predators have managed to survive on isolated islands. One of these is the tuatara, a lizard-like creature found only on some islands off New Zealand. The tuatara is the only living member of a group of reptiles that died out elsewhere

THE KOMODO DRAGON IS A FORMIDABLE PREDATOR, HUNTING ANIMALS SUCH AS PIGS, DEER, AND GOATS. IT HAS EVEN BEEN KNOWN TO ATTACK PEOPLE.

LOG ON...
galapagos/wildlife/intro.html
www.terraquest.com/

about 65 million years ago! It's often described as a "living fossil."

Unique species
Another effect of this isolation is that one form of an animal

MADAGASCAR'S RING-TAILED LEMUR EATS FRUIT, LEAVES, BARK, AND GRASS. IT LIVES IN GROUPS UP TO 30 STRONG.

may develop into a variety of new species to make the most of all the different foods and habitats available. Lemurs, for example, are primates found only on Madagascar, an island off Africa's eastern coast. They arrived about 50 million years ago, and their mainland cousins later became extinct. Today, there are 50 or so different lemur species, all descended from the original colonists.

Famous finches
Without a doubt, the most famous example of this is the finches of the Galapagos. Many thousands of years ago, a flock of seed-eating finches arrived on the islands, probably blown there by a storm. At the time, there were no other insect- or fruit-eating birds on the islands, or birds that weedled out grubs from under tree bark. Over time, the finches developed into different species, all living in different places, with differently shaped beaks to take advantage of the various types of food.

57

There are now 14 species of Galapagos finch, including the woodpecker finch, which didn't bother to change its beak but instead uses a cactus spine to hook grubs from rotten wood!

to the newly formed volcanic islands of Hawaii. Since then, the tarweeds have flourished and evolved into about 30 unique species, from low-lying shrubs to trees 25 ft (7.5 m)

THE SILVERSWORD LIVES FOR 15 YEARS, BUT FLOWERS ONLY ONCE BEFORE IT DIES.

Triumph of the tarweeds

It's not just animals that develop unique island species. Sometime in the distant past, tarweed seeds from California made their way

tall. One of these is the striking silversword, which is found only in Haleakala crater on the Hawaiian island of Maui.

Forgotten how to fly

Some island birds have lost the ability to fly. They include the kakapo, the takahe, and the kiwi, which all come from New Zealand, and the flightless cormorant of the

LIVING ON BOARD SHIPS, RATS WERE ABLE TO SPREAD TO MANY ISLANDS, AS TRADERS AND EXPLORERS SAILED THE WORLD'S OCEANS.

Galapagos. Flying takes up a lot of energy, but it's well worth it if it helps a bird to escape predators or to find food. However, these birds found that food was readily available on their island homes, and that there were no predators to flee from – so why bother to fly?

Fragile success

Island creatures don't get everything their own way. They become vulnerable when humans upset the balance of island life by introducing new species. Animals that can't defend themselves or escape when threatened can be wiped out by carnivores such as cats and dogs. Grazing animals such as goats and rabbits also devour their food sources. And people may hunt the animals for food.

In the 17th century, European sailors visiting the island of

THE FLIGHTLESS KIWI LIVES IN BURROWS. IT IS SOMETIMES PREYED ON BY WILD DOGS, CATS, AND STOATS INTRODUCED BY PEOPLE.

Mauritius in the Indian Ocean exterminated the dodo, a large, flightless pigeon. The dodo was so easy to catch, it made an easy meal. A quick bash on the head, and, hey presto, there's supper! Unable to escape the sailors' appetites, or protect its eggs from the attentions of rats and dogs, the poor dodo soon became extinct.

DEEP-SEA DWELLERS

Down on the deep-ocean floor, it's pitch black and icy cold, and the huge pressure from the water would crush a person like an eggshell! Food is scarce, because plankton – the microscopic plants and animals that nourish creatures near the surface – can't survive at this depth. Huge teeth, strange bodies, and built-in lighting effects help deep-sea dwellers to survive against the odds.

Under pressure

At a depth of 3,280 ft (1,000 m), the pressure is about 100 times greater than it is at the surface. Deep-sea animals (there are no plants because there's no light,

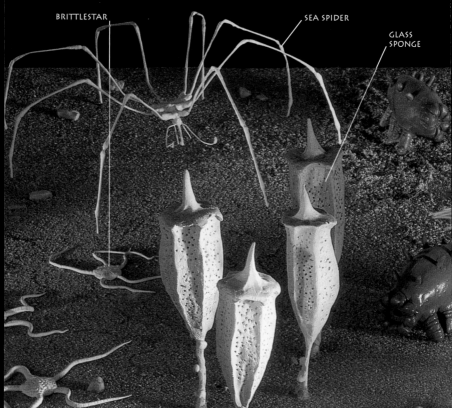

BRITTLESTAR

SEA SPIDER

GLASS SPONGE

so they can't photosynthesize) contain special proteins that help their bodies to work better under extreme pressure. Most also have watery flesh, because liquids resist being compressed.

In the ooze
Many bottom-dwellers feed on the debris (droppings and dead plant and animal remains) that drifts down from above. Sea cucumbers and worms munch through the muddy ooze on the seafloor to extract food particles. Sea pens and glass sponges stand up in the ooze, filtering specks of food from the water around

them. These debris-eaters grow bacteria in their intestines that help them to digest their food.

Mud walkers
To leep from sinking into the mud, some bottom-living fish and crustaceans (such as crabs and shrimp) have long legs or fins to spread their weight over

MOST SEAFLOOR ANIMALS FEED ON DEBRIS FLOATING DOWN FROM ABOVE. OTHER CREATURES FEED ON THESE DEBRIS-EATERS.

SEA PEN

TRIPOD FISH

VENUS FLOWER BASKET SPONGE

THE BLACK SWALLOWER HAS WIDE JAWS AND A VERY STRETCHY BELLY TO COPE WITH LARGE MEALS.

a wide area. The tripod fish has three long, stiff fins to hold its body above the ooze, preventing it from stirring up muddy clouds as it moves over the seabed in search of prey.

Slow growth

Most deep-sea fish are predators. But encounters with prey are few and far between, so they try to minimize energy use between meals. They're usually small, because larger fish wouldn't survive on so little food. Their bodies work slowly, which means that they also grow slowly but tend to live for a long time. To consume less energy when they move, they have lightweight skeletons and body organs. And there's no current to swim against, so they need only a few muscles to push their bodies through the water.

THE BODY OF THE FANGTOOTH IS COVERED WITH PORES THAT CAN DETECT THE MOVEMENTS OF ITS PREY.

Armed to the teeth

Because they're weak swimmers, deep-sea fish don't usually waste energy chasing prey. Most are sit-and-wait hunters, hanging around in the water with mouths agape. They have huge jaws to

sea eel, two bristlemouths, five shrimp, and a hatchet fish in its stomach! Angler fish and some other hunters have a glowing lure, like a fishing rod, which they use to attract prey toward their razor-sharp teeth.

AT 1,970 FT (600 M), THE OCEAN IS IN TOTAL DARKNESS

FLASHLIGHT FISH HAVE A LIGHT ORGAN UNDER EACH EYE. THEY USE "SHUTTERS" OF DARK SKIN TO TURN THEM ON AND OFF.

The light-makers

If you want light down in the depths, you've got to make it yourself! More than half of all deep-sea creatures produce their own light, which is usually bluish in color. They do this with special light organs on the sides of their heads, their flanks, or at the end of a fin. These organs either produce light by chemical reactions or contain colonies of luminous bacteria. The bacteria shine all the time, but some fish can turn their lights on and off by sliding a curtain of skin across the light

gobble up whatever comes their way – regardless of size. Their cavernous jaws are often chock-full of sharp teeth that curve backward to stop their dinner from wriggling free. Many of these scary-looking predators have very stretchy stomachs that can expand to accommodate meals almost as big as themselves. One angler fish was found to have a deep-

63

animals. Here, many creatures have shrunken eyes that can detect little more than light and dark, and some have no eyes at all. They compensate for near or total

organ, or by restricting the supply of blood to the colony.

Glow-in-the dark fish use their lights to keep a shoal of fish together, to dazzle or

THE RAT-TAIL FISH USES ITS FLESHY, BEARDLIKE BARBELS TO DETECT SMALL CREATURES BY TOUCH.

blindness by having organs that are sensitive to touch, or that can detect chemicals in the water. Some deep-sea dwellers and visitors can sense the small electrical currents given off when animal muscles contract.

Others can find prey by echo-location (page 18). Sperm whales, for example, dive to 3,280 ft (1,000 m) as they track down giant squid using echo-location.

confuse predators, or to find a mate or a meal. Fish that swim up to feed in the dimly lit midwaters at night use them as camouflage. Light organs on the underside of their bodies help to break up their silhouette, making it harder for predators to spot them from below.

Senses in the darkness

Down in the murky depths, the only light comes from these luminous

Cling-on fish

Finding a mate is not easy in the inky blackness, so when a male angler fish finds a female, he makes

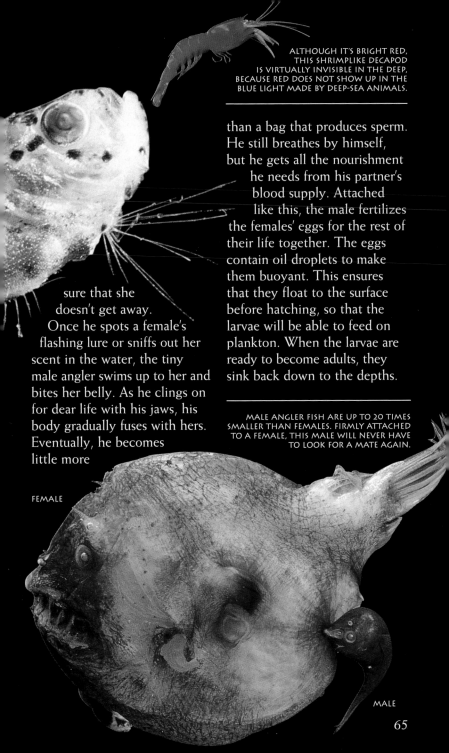

than a bag that produces sperm. He still breathes by himself, but he gets all the nourishment he needs from his partner's blood supply. Attached like this, the male fertilizes the females' eggs for the rest of their life together. The eggs contain oil droplets to make them buoyant. This ensures that they float to the surface before hatching, so that the larvae will be able to feed on plankton. When the larvae are ready to become adults, they sink back down to the depths.

sure that she doesn't get away.
Once he spots a female's flashing lure or sniffs out her scent in the water, the tiny male angler swims up to her and bites her belly. As he clings on for dear life with his jaws, his body gradually fuses with hers. Eventually, he becomes little more

FEMALE

MALE

VENT TUBEWORMS ARE PACKED WITH
BACTERIA, WHICH SUPPLY THE WORMS
WITH NOURISHING CHEMICALS.

Hydrothermal vents

By now you'll have realized that
the deep ocean is a pretty weird
place. On the seafloor, over
6,560 ft (2,000 m) below the
waves, strange communities of
animals cluster around features
called hydrothermal vents. The
vents occur where subterranean
rocks heat water seeping down
through cracks in the seafloor.
Clouds of superheated water, at
temperatures of 662°F (350°C)
or more, then shoot back out of
the cracks, carrying minerals
dissolved from the rocks. These
mineral-rich clouds look like
smoke, and they emerge from
chimneylike structures formed
from deposited minerals.

Bacteria thrive on the warmth
here and use sulfide minerals
from the water as a source of
energy. They, in turn, provide
food for animals such as crabs,
anemones, mussels,
giant clams, and
tubeworms.
These vent
animals occur in
abundance, and
many grow
unusually large.
Tubeworms, for
example, may
reach up to
10 ft (3 m) long.

VENT CHIMNEYS
TOWER 50–65 FT
(15–20 M))
ABOVE THE
SEA FLOOR.

Hydrothermal vents were only discovered 25 years ago, and scientists are still trying to understand how vent communities survive. The vents have a limited lifespan – perhaps 50 years – so what happens to the animals when the "chimneys" stop smoking? It may be that the vent animals produce tiny larvae that swim off to other vents far away. But exactly how they find the new vents is one of many mysteries waiting to be solved by deep-sea explorers. At the moment, we probably know more about the Moon than the Earth's deep oceans!

IN THE DARK

Eyes like saucers, enormous ears, and long feelers – special sensors such as these help animals to survive at night or in dark caves and murky burrows. For us, the darkness is a world of mysterious shadows and scary sounds. But many animals prefer it. In the gloom, they can hide from predators or sneak up on prey. They can even find shelter from the heat of the sun.

A TAWNY OWL CAN SPOT ITS PREY IN SURROUNDINGS THAT ARE 100 TIMES DARKER THAN THOSE IN WHICH WE CAN SEE.

Creatures of the night

In any habitat, more animals can survive if some are active at night and others during the day. This balances the competition for food and space. For example, Douroucoulis (night monkeys) feed on fruit at night while other monkeys sleep. If the Douroucoulis came out in the day, fiercer monkeys would steal their food.

Some hunters have adapted to use the darkness to their own advantage, so that they can prey on these night creatures. Owls, for example, have superb hearing and soft, fringed feathers that help them to fly ultraquietly as they search for unsuspecting victims. Much bigger and more dangerous night hunters – to us, anyway! – are large cats, such as lions, tigers, and leopards. Their spongy footpads help them to walk so quietly that prey animals have no idea that they're about to be pounced on – and eaten.

Thin skin
In warm climates, many animals are nocturnal (active at night) because it enables them to avoid the heat of the day. To a thin-skinned animal that must stay moist to survive – such as a slug, frog, or gecko (a type of small lizard) – the hot daytime air is a disaster. Only when it gets cooler after sunset can such animals find relief from the drying air that would sentence them to death by dehydration.

One animal that you might think would be thick-skinned enough for the hot sun is the hippopotamus. Surprisingly, hippos can get sunburned!

IN WARM PLACES, GECKOS ARE OFTEN FOUND IN HOUSES AT NIGHT. THEY CLING TO WALLS AND CEILINGS WITH THEIR ADHESIVE FOOTPADS.

They spend the day wallowing in mud or water to keep their skin damp and cool. At night, they emerge to chomp their way through vast quantities of greenery.

Night vision
How do animals find their way in the dark? Well, the night isn't always pitch black – there's usually some light from the moon and stars. The eyes of birds called nightjars are very good at seeing in this dim light. They can make out the faint silhouettes of their flying insect prey against the night sky.

Many night animals, such as owls and tarsiers (small South-East Asian monkeys), have big eyes, with large pupils and lenses to let in as much light as possible. In one species of tarsier, a single eye can weigh more than the animal's brain! The eyes of tarsiers and owls are so big that they can't move in their sockets.

To make up for this, they can turn their heads completely around to see behind them.

Some animals that are active at night, such as cats, have a built-in mirror, called a tapetum, at the back of the eye. It reflects light from the rear of the eye toward the front again. The light passes through the eye twice, so the animal sees an image that's twice as bright.

Deep down inside caves, it is completely dark, and eyesight is of little use. Cave fish and cave salamanders are blind, but they are guided by an acute sense of touch and smell, and an ability to sense vibrations.

Seeing without eyes
Some snakes, such as pit vipers, boas, and pythons, can "see" in the dark without using their eyes. To make up for their poor vision, they have special organs on their heads called heat pits. These can detect the body heat given off by warm-blooded animals, allowing the snakes to find prey in total darkness

Noises in the night
The night can be full of shrieks, squeaks, and croaks, as animals call out to one another. Some of the calls are to attract mates, others to ward off rivals.

Large flexible ears, such as

MOST NOCTURNAL ANIMALS CAN SEE ONLY IN BLACK AND WHITE

GOOD EYESIGHT ISN'T EVERYTHING – PIT VIPERS CAN DETECT THE BODY HEAT OF THEIR PREY USING SPECIAL HEAT PITS IN FRONT OF THEIR EYES.

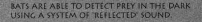

BATS ARE ABLE TO DETECT PREY IN THE DARK USING A SYSTEM OF "REFLECTED" SOUND.

those of foxes, rabbits, and bats, are good at funneling sounds into the ear. Some animals can even swivel their ears to pinpoint the direction from which a sound is coming.

Many bats locate prey in the dark by "shouting" at it. They make high-pitched squeaks and listen for the echoes that bounce off insects and back to their ears. It's similar to the way that sperm whales hunt squid (page 64), and it enables the bats to detect objects as small as a human hair. So that they don't deafen themselves, they "switch off" their ears for the brief time it takes to make each squeak.

Smells in the air

Many night animals use their sense of smell to find food or mates, or to detect danger. Female moths give off powerful scents that the males can pick up far away with their antennae. A male emperor moth can smell potential mates from as far away as 6.8 miles (11 km). Dung beetles, too, have a nifty sense of smell. They can detect the delicious aroma of fresh cow

WEIRD WORLD
YOUNG CAVE FISH ARE USUALLY BORN WITH EYES, BUT SKIN GROWS OVER THE EYES AT ABOUT 13 DAYS OLD. AFTER 52 DAYS, BOTH EYES ARE COMPLETELY HIDDEN.

and sheep dung many miles downwind.

Birds usually rely more on their eyes and ears than their sense of smell. But two night birds, the kiwi and the oilbird, are exceptions. The kiwi detects worms and insects on the forest floor with nostrils right at the tip of its bill, while oilbirds use nostrils higher up the beak to sniff out tasty fruit.

Touchy feely

The sense of touch is very important to night creatures, and can make all the difference between eating and being eaten. Long whiskers enable some animals to feel obstacles close to them as they move about. Naked mole rats, which live underground, have touch-sensitive hairs on their bodies to help them find their way around their burrows. Likewise, spiders use their hairy legs to

pick up the vibrations made when insect prey blunders into their webs at night. And the long antennae of cave cockroaches and cave crickets – which can be up to three times their body length – enable them to find food and avoid predators in their murky cave homes.

Lures of light

Like deep-ocean creatures, a few animals produce their own light using chemical reactions inside their bodies. The larvae of some fungus gnat flies live in tubes of mucus suspended from cave ceilings. They dangle long, sticky threads of silk from their tubes and wave their glowing tails around. Shimmering in the light, the threads attract flying insects that become entangled in the sticky threads. The larvae then reel in the threads and feast on their captives.

Lights in the darkness can also be used to find romance. Firefly beetles attract mates with flashes of light from organs on their abdomens. Each species has its own pattern of flashes so that individuals can recognize fireflies of their own kind. Some females have another, more macabre use for their light organs. They copy the flashing patterns of other species, and devour any unfortunate males who arrive looking for love!

Owls also sometimes glow in the dark – but not deliberately. It happens when luminous fungi get caught in their feathers. So if you see a glowing owl on a dark night, it's not trying to lure you to your doom!

NAKED MOLE RATS
LIVE IN COMPLETE
DARKNESS IN BURROWS.
THEY HAVE WHISKERS, AS
WELL AS TOUCH-SENSITIVE
HAIRS ALL OVER THEIR BODIES.

THE URBAN JUNGLE

Animals have had millions of years to adapt to Earth's natural habitats, but only a few thousand years to adjust to life in cities. But those that aren't fussy eaters, don't mind the noise or bright lights, and are quick to make the most of opportunities, can find that built-up areas have a lot to offer. And for some creatures, the urban jungle has some surprising similarities to their natural habitats…

Nesting city-style

Plants tend to take root wherever there's spare ground. But apart from parks and gardens, our modern cities don't at first glance appear to have many suitable places for animals to set up home and raise their young.

Despite this, some animals have discovered that the buildings and structures of urban environments provide nesting places that resemble those in their natural habitats.

> ### WEIRD WORLD
> IN 1890–91, ABOUT 100 STARLINGS WERE RELEASED INTO CENTRAL PARK IN NEW YORK CITY. TODAY, 110 YEARS LATER, THERE ARE MORE THAN 50 MILLION STARLINGS IN NORTH AMERICA!

To some peregrine falcons, for example, windowsills and roofs on high buildings seem like the cliff ledges they nest on in the wild. The chimney swift, a bird that once built its nest inside hollow trees, now nests happily in chimneys and ventilator shafts, which offer the same shelter and protection.

Bats find that nesting in attics is just like nesting in caves, while rats inhabit drains and sewers – the urban equivalent of holes in riverbanks. Foxes may give birth to their cubs under the floors of houses. Such spaces are dry and warm, like the dens they make in the wild, and there's room for the cubs to play in safety.

Cold-store critters

Mice often live in cavities between walls, but they'll try anywhere – including in sacks of grain or flour, and even in meat cold stores, where it may be colder than $16°F$ $(-9°C)$.

These meat-freezer mice have developed thicker fur to cope

AT A SEASIDE TOWN, A MASS OF STARLINGS
FLOCKS TO A PIER AT DUSK TO KEEP WARM.

with their chilly lodgings. They
gnaw holes in frozen carcasses
to make their nests, and line
them with scraps of cloth used
for wrapping meat. Content
in the cooler, the mice
have no need
for the next
benefit
of urban
living –
extra heat.

THIS RACCOON
HAS KNOCKED
OVER A GARBAGE
CAN IN SEARCH OF
SOMETHING TO
MUNCH ON.

Heat from the streets

Cities are often several degrees
warmer than the surrounding
countryside, especially at night.
This warmth comes partly from
heated homes, offices, and
factories, but also from the way
that buildings and pavements
absorb heat from
the sun during
the day, and
then release
it into the
air again
at night.

In cold weather, birds such as starlings often flock to cities at dusk to enjoy this urban heat during their night-time roost. The city's warmth also allows animals like rats and pigeons to breed all year round. What's more, central heating has enabled creatures such as cockroaches, which originally lived in warm climates, to spread across the globe.

Even muck can be an urban lifesaver in winter. The heat given off by rotting materials on compost heaps and garbage dumps helps to keep

SOME CITIES CONTAIN AS MANY RATS AS THEY DO PEOPLE

alive lizards, crickets, and slow-worms that wriggle under the festering piles. Snakes may also lay their eggs in rotting garbage where the warmth speeds up the development of the eggs.

Successful scavengers
Many urban animals dine well on the crumbs we spill and on our discarded fast-food meals.

Raccoons and foxes are expert at rifling through garbage cans for edible scraps. (Some raccoons have been known to walk into kitchens and raid the fridge!) Of course, the food's very different from their diet in the wild, but they've developed broad tastes to make the most of what's on the urban menu. Other garbage gobblers include storks, gulls,

hyenas, opossums, vultures, rats, and jackals. Even polar bears have found that Arctic garbage dumps are so full of tasty tidbits that they're worth a visit.

The wider the range of things an animal eats, the greater its chance of survival. One reason that mice are so good at city living is that they'll eat almost anything. They've even been known to munch on such oddities as soap, string, paper, and candle wax!

COWS ROAM FREELY THROUGH THE STREETS OF TOWNS AND CITIES IN INDIA.

different matter when animals devour our homes. The larvae (grubs) of woodworm beetles once lived in the bark of old trees. Now they chew their way

E at my house!
We may not mind our waste being eaten, but it's a

THIS MOUSE IS GNAWING THROUGH AN ELECTRIC CABLE.

LOG ON...
~rmaurizi/urban.html
www.uvm.edu/

through wooden furniture and house timbers, often reducing them to dust. Termites cause similar chaos in tropical regions.

Population explosions

So, you see, many animals can make a good living alongside us in the urban jungle. In fact, pigeons and house sparrows are now so well adapted to urban life that they're rarely seen elsewhere. But if urban animals do too well, their numbers may increase so dramatically that they become pests. Some, such as rats, cockroaches, and pigeons, carry diseases, so city authorities need to keep them in check.

It doesn't help that there are few predators in urban areas. Peregrine falcons prey on city pigeons, while feral cats (pet cats that have run wild) help to make a dent in the populations of rats and mice. But a single pair of rats and their offspring can have 15,000 young a year, so it's an uphill battle.

To control the numbers of "pest" animals, city authorities often use chemicals that either poison them or prevent them from breeding. However, animal bodies are very adaptable, and they often build up resistance to the chemicals after a time.

Special privileges

Not all urban animals get such rough treatment. In India, cows and monkeys are considered sacred by followers of the Hindu religion, so they are respected, fed, and given special protection. In fact, there are probably more monkeys living in India's cities than there are in its forests!

PEREGRINE FALCONS PERCH ON HIGH BUILDINGS, AND THEN SWOOP DOWN TO SNATCH PIGEONS IN MIDAIR.

SURVIVING PEOPLE

The biggest survival challenge facing plants and animals today is coping with human interference. The world's human population has doubled in the last 40 years – by the mid-21st century, there may be 9 billion of us. We have taken over most of the planet, destroyed wild places, and polluted the air, water, and soil. It's tough for wildlife now, but it's likely to get even tougher in the future.

Home wreckers

Habitat destruction is a huge threat to wildlife – if plants and animals have nowhere to live, they can't survive. There's no more important wildlife "home" than the rain forests, where half of all the Earth's known plant and animal species live. In one acre, there may be 200 species of tree, hundreds of different mammals, reptiles, amphibians, and birds, and thousands of insects. But rain forests are being felled at an alarming rate for timber, and to free up land for farming, mining, and other uses.

Wildlife is more closely linked in rain forests than in any other habitat, with each species aiding the survival of others. Take the bromeliad plant, for example,

A BROMELIAD'S SHAPE CHANNELS FALLEN FRUIT AND LEAVES INTO A POOL IN THE CENTER OF THE PLANT, WHERE THEY ROT TO PROVIDE IT WITH NUTRIENTS.

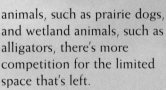

which grows high on rain forest trees. Rain collects in its center, and this treetop swimming pool is home to insects, worms, and snails. Frogs visit the pools to lay their eggs. So if a bromeliad dies, lots of animals die, too. And when a rain forest tree is cut down, the hundreds of plants and animals that rely on the tree for survival also perish.

Pollution problem

In addition to destroying rain forests, people have plowed up grasslands and drained wetlands to grow crops. For grassland

HALF OF THE WORLD'S RAIN FORESTS HAVE NOW BEEN DESTROYED. AT PRESENT RATES OF DESTRUCTION, ALL THE RAIN FORESTS COULD BE GONE WITHIN ABOUT 40 YEARS.

animals, such as prairie dogs, and wetland animals, such as alligators, there's more competition for the limited space that's left.

You'd think that, desert peoples aside, humans would leave deserts alone because they are so hot and dry. But even here, they drive cars and motorcycles for sport,

damaging the fragile desert soils and destroying plants that desert animals need to survive.

To date, the Antarctic and Arctic have suffered least at the hands of humans because the weather is so extreme that it's difficult for people to live there. But the impact of humans is beginning to be felt. Pipelines carry oil and gas across the Arctic tundra, obstructing migration routes that caribou have followed for thousands of years. And growing numbers of tourists disturb polar wildlife and pollute the landscape with their waste. Meanwhile, global warming (caused by emissions from cars, factories, and power stations) is melting the polar ice, threatening the future of many animals, from polar bears to penguins.

400 DIFFERENT TYPES OF INSECT LIVE ON ONE RAIN FOREST TREE

P ollution perils

All over the planet, wildlife is at risk from pollution. Coral reefs need clean water to survive, but coastal building sites churn out fine mud, called silt, which may drain into the sea and smother the coral. Rising sea temperatures, as a result of global warming, may also be upsetting the delicate balance of life on coral reefs. Oil spills from tankers can cause irreparable damage to sea creatures, including

CORAL REEFS ARE HOME TO A RICH VARIETY OF WILDLIFE.

LOG ON...
www.worldwildlife
.org/fun/kids.cfm

AFTER AN OIL
SPILL, OILY
SEABIRDS MAY
BE CLEANED UP
WITH SOAPY
WATER. SOME
GET TOO THICKLY
COVERED TO SURVIVE.

particularly affected by
"acid rain," which is produced
when polluting gases mix with
rainwater. This can change
the acidity of soils and lakes,
with lethal consequences for
trees and fish in the area.

Pollution also creates holes in
the ozone layer – the band of
ozone gas in the atmosphere
that filters out many of the
ultraviolet rays from sunlight.
Without this protection, these
harmful rays can damage plant
and animal cells.

birds and otters. A seabird with
oily, matted feathers cannot
dive underwater to catch fish
and is no longer protected from
the cold and wet. It may also
be poisoned if it swallows oil.

We are polluting the air as
well as the water. Some trees
cannot thrive in polluted areas,
because the breathing holes
on their leaves
become clogged
with dirt.
Conifer
trees are

F uture survival
But there's plenty we can do to
help plants and
animals to
live

EVERYDAY LITTER
CAN ENDANGER THE
LIVES OF ANIMALS.
THIS HEDGEHOG IS
CAUGHT UP IN SOME
PLASTIC PACKAGING.

alongside us in the future. We can clean up our act by causing less pollution. And by recycling materials and using the Earth's limited resources wisely, we can reduce the need to destroy more wild places. We can pass laws that prevent animals from being hunted for their meat, fur, or skin, and from being taken from the wild by collectors. We can also limit tourism and leisure activities that disturb wildlife.

S eeds of hope

Scientists have set up seed banks, where plant seeds are preserved so that species can be saved from extinction. And most governments have created national parks and nature preserves, where plants and animals can live and

reproduce safely in their natural habitats. Some endangered animals are bred in zoos and then released back into the wild.

Such measures have already saved numerous animals from extinction, from the Arabian oryx (a desert antelope) to the golden lion tamarin monkey. So, there's hope for the future – if people are ready to take up the survival challenge.

IN 1980, ONLY 100 GOLDEN LION TAMARINS WERE LEFT IN THE WILD. THANKS TO THE CREATION OF A NATURE PRESERVE AND BREEDING IN ZOOS, THERE ARE NOW OVER 1,000.

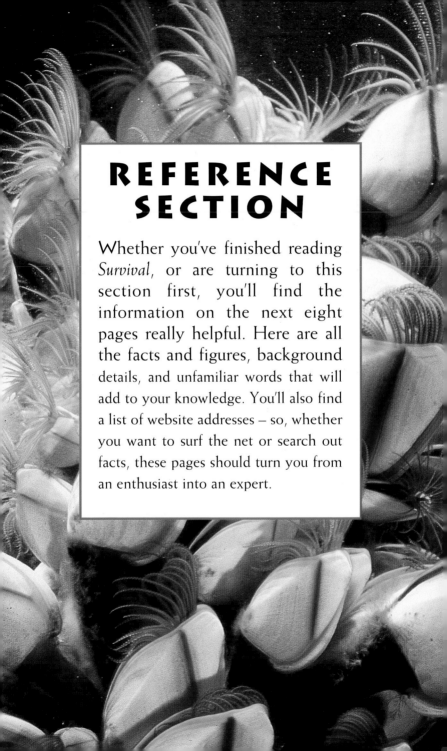

REFERENCE SECTION

Whether you've finished reading *Survival*, or are turning to this section first, you'll find the information on the next eight pages really helpful. Here are all the facts and figures, background details, and unfamiliar words that will add to your knowledge. You'll also find a list of website addresses – so, whether you want to surf the net or search out facts, these pages should turn you from an enthusiast into an expert.

ENDANGERED SPECIES

The Red List of the International Union for the Conservation of Nature (IUCN) currently lists more than 11,000 wildlife species at risk of extinction. It includes 5,485 animals and 5,611 plants.

THE FIVE MOST CRITICALLY ENDANGERED SPECIES IN THE WORLD ARE:
Chinese alligator *(Alligator sinensis)*
Found in wetlands along lower parts of the Yangtze River.
Bonin fruit bat *(Pteropus pselaphon)*
Lives only on five small and remote Japanese islands.
Brazilian guitarfish *(Rhinobatos horkeli)*
A type of ray found along Brazil's southern coast. Its numbers fell by 96 percent between 1984 and 1994.
Philippine eagle *(Pithecophaga jefferyi)*
Only 350–650 birds of this species are left in the Philippines.
Kouprey *(Bos sauveli)*
Less than 250 individuals of this oxlike animal survive in Southeast Asia.

OTHER THREATENED SPECIES INCLUDE:
Iberian lynx *(Lynx pardinus)*
Probably only about 600 survive, mainly in Spain.
Alabama canebrake pitcher plant *(Sarracenia rubra alabamensis)*
Only about 1,600 plants remain in Alabama.
Mandrinette *(Hibiscus fragilis)*
Red-flowered shrub found on the island of Mauritius. About 46 plants remain.
Tibetan antelope or "chiru" *(Pantholops hodgsonii)*
Found on a Tibetan plateau in China and in small areas of northern India and western Nepal. Numbers could be as low as 65,000.
Giant Brazilian otter *(Pteronura brasiliensis)*
Found in rain forests and wetlands of South America.
Cross river gorilla *(Gorilla gorilla diehli)*
Only about 150–200 individuals remain, on the Nigeria-Cameroon border.
Hector's dolphin *(Cephalorhynchus hectori)*
Found only in New Zealand waters.
Fossa *(Cryptoprocta ferox)*
A type of mongoose found in the rain forests of Madagascar, with a population of less than 2,500 mature individuals.
Sturgeon *(Acipenseriformes)*
Threatened by poaching and overfishing in Eastern Europe, Black Sea, and Caspian regions.
Agarwood *(Aquilaria malaccensis)*
Tree threatened by the use of resin from its wood in traditional medicines.

SURVIVAL FACTS AND FEATS

Freezer facts
• The wooly bear caterpillar of the Arctic can spend as much as 10 months of the year frozen solid at temperatures that drop to –58°F (–50°C) or lower.
• Male Antarctic emperor penguins cope with temperatures of –76°F (–60°C) and icy winds of up to 124 mph (200 kmh) while incubating their eggs.
• The blubber of the blowhead whale is 17–20 in (43–50 cm) thick – thicker than in any other animal.
• Antarctic ice fish have more blood than other bony fish, and a heart three times as big which beats up to 10 times as fast.
• Lichens in the Antarctic grow only 0.6 in (15 mm) every 100 years.

High-rise heroes
• The Alpine chough holds the record for the highest roost of all birds – 23,000 ft (7,000 m) up in the Himalayas near Mount Everest.
• The common toad has been found living at 26,250 ft (8,000 m) in the Himalayas – beating the efforts of the large-eared pika, the world's highest-living mammal, which reaches altitudes of up to 20,100 ft (6,130 m).

Hot stuff
• The maximum body temperature that most animals are able to tolerate is 113–122°F (45–50°C). The Pompeii worm survives in water as hot as 176°F (80°C) around hydrothermal vents on the ocean floor. Some bacteria thrive in temperatures of 235°F (113°C) around vents in the Pacific Ocean!

Defying drought
• The most drought-resistant tree is the African baobab, which can store up to 29,920 gallons (136,000 liters) of water in its trunk.
• North America's spadefoot toad survives drought by burying itself and living off its fat reserves. It can stay alive like this for up to nine months.

Ocean secrets
• The deepest known fish, *Abyssobrotula galatheae*, was found in the Atlantic Ocean's Puerto Rican Trench, at a depth of 27,480 ft (8,376 m). There are also microorganisms, sea cucumbers, and worms that live in the very deepest ocean sediments, more than 34,450 ft (10,500 m) below the surface.

Migration marvels
• Desert locusts migrate in larger numbers than any other land creature. The largest locust swarm recorded contained more than 10 billion insects!
• The biggest migration takes place in the ocean each night, as 1,000 million tons of deep-sea creatures journey up toward the surface to feed.

ANIMAL AND PLANT LIFESPANS

Bristlecone pine	5,000 years	Jewel beetle	30 years plus
Giant sequoia tree	3,200 years	Kangaroo	up to 28 years
Antarctic lichen	2,000 years	Porcupine	27 years
Oak tree	1,500 years	Grizzly bear	25–30 years
Swiss stone pine	750 years	Giraffe	20–25 years
Some turtles	up to 200 years	Bird-eating spider	20–25 years
Saguaro cactus	150 years	Queen ant	15 years
Some crocodiles	up to 100 years	Lion	15 years
Fin whale	90–100 years	Giant anteater	14 years
Cockatoo	over 80 years	Rabbit	6–8 years
Elephant	70–80 years	Armadillo	4 years
Spiny dogfish	over 70 years	Mouse	3 years
Sea anemone	60–90 years	Virginia opossum	1–2 years
Swan	up to 70 years	Worker ant	1 year
Giant salamanders	up to 55 years	Long-tailed shrew	12–18 months
Goldfish	over 50 years	Common poppy	6 months
Gorilla	35–45 years	Adult mayflies	at least 1 hour
Boa constrictor	40 years	Bacteria	at least
Horse	20–40 years		20 minutes

MIGRATION

Animal	Route of migration	Annual distance traveled
Arctic tern	Arctic to Antarctic	25,000 miles (40,000 km)
Golden plover	Canada to Argentina	15,000 miles (24,000 km)
Gray whale	Arctic to California/Korea	11,200 miles (18,000 km)
Barn swallow	Europe to Africa	7,500 miles (12,000 km)
Alaska fur seal	Arctic to Japan/west coast of North America	6,000 miles (9,600 km)
Caribou	Canada to Arctic	5,600 miles (9,000 km)
European eel	Europe to western Atlantic	3,500 miles (5,600 km)
Cuckoo	Europe to Africa or Southeast Asia	2,800–7,500 miles (4,500–12,000 km)
Monarch butterfly	Cananda to Mexico	2,500 miles (4,000 km)
White stork	Europe to Africa	1,240–6,500 miles (2,000–10,500 km)
Demoiselle crane	Siberia to India	930–2,800 miles (1,500–4,500 km)

WILDLIFE HABITATS

POLAR AND TUNDRA

Animals (examples)	Polar bear, musk ox, narwhal, walrus, snowy owl, penguin, Weddell seal, Arctic fox, Arctic tern, albatross, reindeer, moose, wolf.
Plants	Lichen, moss, tussock grass, sundew, Arctic poppy, purple saxifrage, Arctic willow, glacier crowfoot, bilberry.
Climate	Long, cold winters. Short summers.
Temperature	From –76°F (–60°C) in Antarctic winter to 50°F (10°C) in Arctic summer.
Precipitation	10–16 in (10°C) per year, most as snow or ice. Little rain.

MOUNTAIN

Animals	Bighorn sheep, grizzly bear, chinchilla, pika, yak, snow leopard, marmot, llama, golden eagle, Andean condor.
Plants	Edelweiss, saxifrage, gentian, giant groundsel, Alpine snowbell, snow willow, moss, lichen, fir and pine trees.
Climate	Strong winds, thin, dry air, strong sunlight. Cold winters.
Temperature	From 14°F to –58°F (–10°C to –50°C) on mountain peaks, warmer in forests at lower levels.
Precipitation	Up to 16 in (40 cm) per year, most as snow at high altitude.

HOT DESERT

Animals	Fennec fox, camel, sandgrouse, jerboa, sandfish lizard, red kangaroo, scorpion, desert tortoise, vulture, parakeet.
Plants	Saguaro cactus, *Welwitschia*, mesquite tree, creosote bush, ocotillo, pebble plant, date palm, century plant.
Climate	Hot and dry all year round. Nights can be very cold.
Temperature	From 86°F to 120°F (30°C to 49°C) by day. In some deserts, temperatures can drop to 14°F (–10°C) at night.
Precipitation	Less than 25 cm (10 in) of rain per year. There may be no rain at all in some years.

RAIN FOREST

Animals	Spider monkey, jaguar, peccary, toucan, gorilla, Goliath beetle, orangutan, tree kangaroo, tapir.
Plants	Bromeliad, pitcher plant, dipterocarp and mahogany trees, strangler fig, bucket orchid, Swiss-cheese plant, ant plant.
Climate	Hot and wet all year round. The humidity (the moisture content of the air) is always high.
Temperature	From 73°F to 88°F (23°C to 31°C) all year round.
Precipitation	98 in (250 cm) of rain, spread evenly throughout the year.

TEMPERATE FORESTS	
Animals	Porcupine, woodpecker, chipmunk, deer, squirrel, monarch butterfly, honey possum, sugar glider, rosella.
Plants	Bluebell, bramble, honeysuckle, wood anemone, starflower, ivy, fern, fir and pine trees, hazel, maple, beech, oak.
Climate	Warm, humid summers. Cold winters with snowfall. Four distinct seasons per year.
Temperature	From 23°F to 77°F (−5°C to 25°C).
Precipitation	2–6 in (5–15 cm) of rain per year, snow and ice in winter.

GRASSLANDS	
Animals	Ostrich, maned wolf, viscacha, lion, zebra, giraffe, hamster, saiga antelope, gray kangaroo, vulture.
Plants	Pampas grass, goldenrod, prairie crocus, wild onion, pasque flower, Indian paintbrush, baobab and acacia trees.
Climate	Hot dry season followed by a cooler, wet season.
Temperature	From −22°F (−30°C) in winter to 86°F (30°C) in summer.
Precipitation	10–30 in (25–75 cm) of rain per year.

SURVIVAL WEBSITES

www.learn.co.uk/default.asp?WCI=SubUnit&WCU=19563
Educational web page explaining the theory of evolution.
www.bbc.co.uk/learning/library/nature/index.shtml
Click on "World Plants" to find out about the global distribution of plants.
Click on "Animals" in the "Nature Selection" box for excellent animal links.
http://mbgnet.mobot.org/index.htm
Get the lowdown on rain forests, grasslands, tundra, deserts, freshwater
ecosystems, marine ecosystems, and more.
www.fi.edu/tfi/units/life/habitat/habitat.html
This site, from the Franklin Institute, has information and links on the world's
different environments, plus endangered species and extinction.
www.mountainnature.com/Home.htm
Find out about mountains at this site, which explores the wildlife, ecology,
and geology of the Rocky Mountains.
www.onr.navy.mil/focus/ocean/
Website of the Office of Naval Research in the US, with information on
oceans, sea mammals, and habitats such as beaches, estuaries, coral reefs,
and hydrothermal vents.
www.bagheera.com/inthewild/index.html
Endangered species and conservation issues.

GLOSSARY

Acid rain
Rain that is more acidic than normal.
Acid rain occurs when polluting
gases mix with water in the air.

Adaptation
The way in which a plant or animal
changes over many generations to
increase its chances of survival in a
particular habitat.

Aestivation
The deep sleep or lack of movement
used by some animals to survive a
hot, dry summer season.

Algae (singular – alga)
Simple organisms that live like plants
by collecting energy from sunlight.

Amphibian
A cold-blooded animal, such as a
frog, that has a smooth, wet skin and
lives both on land and in the water.

Antarctica
The frozen continent around the
South Pole.

Antennae (singular – antenna)
Long sense organs on the heads of
insects and crustaceans. Antennae
detect vibrations, smells, and tastes.

Arctic
The frozen ocean and lands around
the North Pole.

Bacteria
Microscopic, one-celled organisms.

Blubber
A layer of fat under the skin of
animals that live in cold places.
Blubber helps them to keep warm
and also acts as a food store.

Camouflage
The way that animals use shape and
color to blend in with their
surroundings and hide from view.

Carnivore
A meat-eating animal or plant.

Cells
The smallest units of living matter.
Most animals and plants have
millions of cells, but some organisms,
such as bacteria, have just one.

Cold-blooded
An animal such as a fish, frog, lizard,
or insect, whose body temperature
changes with that of its surroundings.

Colonize
To invade a new habitat and settle
down there.

Crustaceans
An animal without a backbone that
has jointed legs and two pairs of
antennae. Crabs, shrimp, and
woodlice are crustaceans.

Cyst
A protective coating formed around
an animal's body in dry conditions.

Dehydration
The process of losing water.

Desert
A place with very little rainfall, or
even none at all. There are cold
deserts, as well as hot ones.

Digestion
The breaking down of food into
simple chemicals that an animal's
body can absorb.

Echolocation
The way in which some animals
navigate or find prey by making
high-pitched sounds and listening for
the echoes that return to their ears.

Environment
The surroundings of a living thing,
including physical factors, such as air
and water, and other living things.

Evolution
The gradual process by which life develops and changes, and new species appear. Evolution is thought to occur as a result of natural selection.

Extinction
The disappearance of a species, when the last one of its kind dies.

Follicle
A depression in a mammal's skin, from which hair grows.

Food chain
A process in which nutrients pass along a chain of living things. For example, a plant is eaten by an insect, which in turn is eaten by a bird.

Fungi (singular – fungus)
Organisms that absorb food from living or dead matter around them. Fungi reproduce by releasing spores.

Germinate
To sprout.

Gill
An organ for breathing underwater.

Gland
Part of an animal's body that produces natural chemicals to control body processes.

Global warming
The warming of the Earth caused by the pollution of the atmosphere.

Habitat
The natural home of a living thing.

Hibernation
The resting state, like a very deep sleep, that some animals go into to help them survive winter.

Hydrothermal vent
A crack in the deep-ocean floor, from which jets of hot, mineral-rich water escape.

Insulation
Preventing heat loss with a layer such as fur, feathers, or blubber.

Kidney
An organ in an animal's body that removes waste materials from the blood and regulates the amount of water in the body.

Larvae (singular – larva)
Young animals that look very different from their parents, and that live in different ways. Larvae change shape as they grow up.

Lichen
An organism formed by an alga and a fungus living together.

Light organ
An organ on an animal's body that either contains luminous bacteria or produces light by chemical reactions.

Membrane
A thin, skinlike barrier or layer that covers part of an animal or plant, or separates parts of their insides.

Migration
The regular journeys made by some animals to find food, warmth, space, or a place to breed.

Mollusc
A soft-bodied animal without a backbone, often protected by a hard shell. Snails, slugs, squid, and most shellfish are molluscs.

Mucus
A lubricating fluid produced by the bodies of animals.

Natural selection
The theory that the plants and animals best suited to their habitat are the most likely to survive and pass their abilities on to their offspring.

Nutrient
A substance that a living thing needs for growth and to stay healthy.

Oasis
A moist, fertile area in a desert where underground water rises to the surface.

Organ
A self-contained part of a living thing with a special function, such as the brain or the heart.

Organism
Anything that is alive.

Osmosis
The flow of water from a weaker solution to a more concentrated one, through a porous membrane. Osmosis causes fish to lose water from their body fluids to the sea, via their skin.

Ozone layer
A layer of ozone gas in the Earth's atmosphere that filters out many of the Sun's ultraviolet rays.

Parasite
An animal that lives on or in another species, called its host, and feeds off it.

Photosynthesis
A process by which plants use the energy from sunlight to make food from carbon dioxide and water.

Plankton
Tiny plants and animals that drift along near the surface of the sea, and in freshwater.

Pollution
The contamination of air, land, and water by toxic gases and chemicals.

Predator
An animal that hunts other animals for food.

Prey
An animal killed by a predator.

Protein
A substance produced by all cells that is essential for life. Some proteins control chemical processes, others are used as building materials.

Reptile
An animal with a backbone and a dry scaly skin. Snakes, lizards, turtles, and crocodiles are all reptiles.

Respiration
A process by which living things use chemical reactions involving oxygen to release energy from their food.

Salinity
The "saltiness" of a substance, or the amount of salts it contains.

Saliva
A thick fluid produced in or near the mouth to help break down food.

Seasons
Regular changes in the weather throughout the year. Some parts of the world have four seasons – spring, summer, fall, and winter. Others have just a wet and a dry season.

Species
A group of similar living things that can breed with each other.

Spore
A tiny, seedlike package of cells produced by fungi and some plants, such as ferns and mosses.

Tapetum
A reflective layer at the back of some animals' eyes, which enables them to see better at night.

Tentacle
A long, flexible, armlike structure on the heads of some animals without backbones.

Tundra
A cold, largely treeless area, found around Polar regions.

Ultraviolet rays
The rays in sunlight that cause people to tan. Exposure to too many ultraviolet rays can harm living things.

Warm-blooded
An animal (a bird or a mammal) that can keep its body at the same warm temperature all the time. It does this by breaking down food or stored body fat to produce heat.

INDEX

CREDITS

Dorling Kindersley would like to thank:

Dean Price for jacket design and Chris Bernstein for the index.

Additional photography by:

Peter Anderson, Geoff Brightling, Jane Burton, Gables, Philip Gatward, Steve Gorton, Frank Greenaway, Peter Greenaway, Alan Hills, Dave King, Cyril Laubscher, Michael Spencer, Kim Taylor, Jerry Young.

Models made by:

Peter Minister, Gary Staab.

Picture Credits

The publishers would like to thank the following for their kind permission to reproduce copyright photographs:
a=above; b=below; c=center; l=left; r=right; t=top

Bryan and Cherry Alexander Photography: Hans Reinhard 16–17.
Ardea London Ltd: Liz Bomford 20–21; Eric Dragesco 23–4, 23tl; Jean–Paul Ferrero 18t, 27, 40t; Francois Gohier 14; Chris Harvey 83t; Chris Knights 40–1; D. Parer & Parer-Cook 1, 39b; Peter Steyn 38tl; David & Kate Urry 41tr; M. Watson 16t, 26; Andrey Zvoznikov 21tr.
Nature Picture Library: Jurgen Freund 54–55; Pete Oxford 48–9; Peter Scoones 50b; David Shale 62b, 64–5.
Bruce Coleman Ltd: Fred Bruemmer 22, 32t, 70; Carol Hughes 35r; Dr. Eckart Pott 33br, 75t; Natural Selection Inc 42–3; Orion Press 74–5; Pacific Stock 12; Kim Taylor 49t, 77.

Corbis: 51; Dave G. House 28–9; W. Wayne Lockwood 24b, 25b; Jose McDonald 29.
DK Picture Library: Jerry Young 84.
Natural Visions: Jason Venus 8–9.
N.H.P.A.: 4, 83b; B. & C. Alexander 3, 15t; Stephen Dalton 69tr, 78b; Brian Hawkes 20t; Daniel Heuclin 31b; Rich Kirchner 24tr; T. Kitchen & V. Hurst 76b; Stephen Kraseman 58; Kevin Schafer 23b; John Shaw 28b; Norbert Wu 18–19, 45br, 62t, 63, 65b; James Warwick 76t.
Oxford Scientific Films: Dennis Green 47; Howard Hall 46t.
Stefan Podhorodecki: 56, 70–71.
Science Photo Library: Professor N. Russell 13b.

Book Jacket Credits
Front cover:
Still Pictures.

All other images
© Dorling Kindersley Limited.

For further information see:
www.dkimages.com